MW00957853

JOURNEY TO ITHAKA

Memoirs of an American Diplomat

For Christine
May your life Journey
be as exciting and
interesting as mine —

Dave Grimland

November 21, 2017

DAVE GRIMLAND

ISBN: 978-1-4834-3402-5 (sc)
ISBN: 978-1-4834-3403-2 (e)

Library of Congress Control Number: 2015910396

Because of the dynamic nature of the Internet, any web addresses or links contained in this book may have changed since publication and may no longer be valid. The views expressed in this work are solely those of the author and do not necessarily reflect the views of the publisher, and the publisher hereby disclaims any responsibility for them.

Lulu Publishing Services rev. date: 07/28/2015

To Michael, Debra, Scott, Joshua, and Hannah.
May your own journeys be long and full of adventures.
And to Kathleen, for our journey together.

As you set out for Ithaka
hope your road is a long one,
full of adventure, full of discovery.

—Constantine P. Cavafy
"Ithaka"

CONTENTS

Foreword...xi
Acknowledgments.. xiii
Preface: Starting a Workday with a Coup xv

Greece
Chapter 1:   A Sioux in Greece.. 1
Chapter 2:   Relevance of Strabo Today............................... 14
Chapter 3:   Koutouki 16
Chapter 4:   Of Monks and Lobsters 22
Chapter 5:   The Holy Land: Church, Politics ... and
             Tradition 28

Cyprus, Part 1: Before the Coup
Chapter 6:   A Quiet Time of Meditation and Prayer 37
Chapter 7:   The Paris of the Middle East 50

**Cyprus, Part 2: The Coup, Riots,
and an Assassination**
Chapter 8:   How Quickly a Coup Can Change Life............. 61
Chapter 9:   Saving an Old Ship..65
Chapter 10: Our First Riot—and Our First Deaths 74
Chapter 11: Riots: an Almost Daily "Entertainment"..........79
Chapter 12: Flying the Friendly Foreign Service Skies........87
Chapter 13: A Continuing Journey to Ithaka 96

Turkey

Chapter 14: Misadventures in Istanbul 101
Chapter 15: Finding Farouk 107
Chapter 16: "Only One of Us Can Sing, Mr.
President ... and I'm the One on Stage" 115

Bangladesh

Chapter 17: Ready, Aim ... Recite! 123
Chapter 18: The Kindness of Strangers 130
Chapter 19: Bloodsuckers' Delight 136
Chapter 20: Father Charlie: A Pennsylvania Irishman
in Rural Bangladesh 143

India

Chapter 21: Sleeping with a Sikh in Calcutta 155
Chapter 22: Calcutta 162
Chapter 23: An Introduction to Kemal 169
Chapter 24: Landing in New Delhi: Wheels Up or
Wheels Down? 184
Chapter 25: Speaking Truth to Power 189

Afterword: The Road to Ithaka Continues:
Islam in Plentywood, Montana 197
Notes 203

FOREWORD

I learned of the poem "Ithaka," by the nineteenth century Greek poet Constantine Cavafy, soon after I arrived in Athens. Since I frequently heard it recited in social gatherings, I soon worked out a rough translation, and it became obvious that this was "my" poem, something by which I wanted to live. And "Ithaka" still resonates with me.

Its message is simple: the journey and the road that take us toward our transient goals are truly everything for all of us. The goal merely provides an excuse for the journey, and the lessons learned through discovery, adventure, and misadventures are the most powerful.

ACKNOWLEDGMENTS

I am indebted to the following people who have helped turn my memories into memoirs:

- My wife, Kathleen Ralph, for her insistence that I turn these after-dinner anecdotes into stories and who then became my first and best proofreader.
- Halit Refiğ, "the John Ford" of Turkey, who took me on early in my time in Istanbul and served as mentor and friend for over twenty-five years, until his death in October 2009, helping me understand Turkish history and contemporary society, as well as its role in the contemporary Middle East.
- My many friends: Linda Halstead-Acharya, Bharat Acharya, Karen Swartz, and several former staff members in Cyprus, Turkey, Bangladesh, and India who contributed their time and creativity in suggesting details, correcting content and foreign language errors, and, most importantly, offering their friendly encouragement. Some of these folks have lived or traveled in one or more of the countries, but at least one had never set foot outside of the United States: Connie Green, a senior cashier at our local supermarket in Columbus, Montana, has been an enthusiastic reader of numerous chapters, and I have, without her permission, dubbed her "President of the Dave Grimland Book Fan

Club" for her sincere and excited compliments on some of the drafts.

- My first editor, Zena Beth McGlashan, who did what an editor is supposed to do: telling me with her customary honesty what she thought was wrong or right about my writing and improving its flow and storytelling qualities.
- Russell Rowland, who, with his outstanding manuscript formatting and editorial help, turned thirty-six separate stories into a coherent progression of educational adventures and discoveries. Russ teaches a course in creative writing in Billings and is a published author on the literature of the northern Great Plains.
- Sally Kellock, a longtime friend who has lived in many countries while working for UNICEF, who carefully edited the final manuscript.
- Finally, but very importantly, my friend Becky Davis, who donated numerous hours of patient help in helping me switch from Microsoft software to a new Apple machine (which was obviously smarter than me).

In spite of all this help, there may remain errors of fact, and they are entirely my own.

PREFACE

Starting a Workday with a Coup

I was in my downtown office in Nicosia, Cyprus, preparing for a meeting in the American Embassy, twenty minutes away in the city's suburbs. It was about 9:00 a.m., and it took me a few moments to realize that the noise I heard was not a string of firecrackers; bullets were being fired.

I reached for the phone to call the embassy to find out what was happening, but the line was dead. And because this was July 1974, there were no cell phones with texting or tweeting. Our only other communication with the embassy was a two-way radio for emergencies. It lay in its charging cradle, locked in my desk. I tried it but got only static.

Since this was a workday, my American secretary was there as well as our full staff of fifteen Greek and Turkish Cypriots. What was happening? Where exactly was the shooting? Were our families safe? What should we do? No one knew the answers, and we were completely out of touch with anyone who could tell us. As public affairs officer, I felt utterly impotent. This terrifying and tragic incident ended well for us but not for our ambassador, who was killed. That story is told in chapter 10.

The tragic events that unfolded in Cyprus in 1974 were just one piece in the tapestry of my foreign service life. This book contains other stories about my twenty-eight years serving as a diplomat for the United States. Some are funny; some are sad, but all, I hope, are entertaining and informative. They provide glimpses into other cultures and, hopefully, new perspectives on some vexing old problems.

This book is arranged in roughly chronological order, grouped by the countries in which I served: Greece, Cyprus, Turkey, Bangladesh, and India, from 1967 to 1995.

US Foreign Service

It will be helpful to know more about the US Foreign Service. Understandably, most Americans are only vaguely aware of the diplomatic service. If an American abroad loses her passport, the answer to her predicament is to call the embassy. Expert help will be available, of course, but there's much more to the foreign service.

My career in the US Foreign Service, often called the diplomatic service, was entirely concerned with public affairs work. Public affairs is the art of making your company or its products look appealing. For foreign service officers, our employer was the United States government, and our "products" were the foreign policies of whatever administration was in power. Even if we couldn't "sell" them, we were obliged to try to explain them. Given our system of an executive branch often at odds with the legislative branch, this was sometimes a challenge. We were also tasked with presenting a favorable image of American society in general.

Foreign service covers a broad spectrum of Americans working in US embassies and consulates abroad, collectively known as foreign service officers (FSOs). Although most of these people are under the State Department, separate US agencies in Washington, DC, assign their own specialists to countries where they have interests. The US Agency for International Development, for example, has officers who specialize in making recommendations and assisting in long-term development projects. Commercial officers promote US business opportunities. Various US intelligence agencies, as part of US Department of State assignments, provide trained personnel to collect information about the players and policies of the local power structure.

State Department FSOs provide consular services: visas to foreigners wishing to visit the United States and assistance to Americans who have medical, legal, or financial difficulties in the geographic areas covered by a consulate or embassy. State Department personnel also specialize in economic, political, and commercial analysis and reporting. Administrative sections take care of housing, office facilities, embassy security, and changing lightbulbs for the folks who find that too challenging, as is sometimes the case with "bayonet" lightbulbs and different electrical systems.

Generally, the heads of agencies or the senior officers in each section represented in the embassies are expected to attend weekly country team meetings to update the other section heads on concerns or opportunities and to discuss instructions from Washington.

The number of US agencies with special needs abroad can be surprising. The Social Security Administration, for example, often has to track down local citizens who worked in the United States long enough to qualify for benefits, making sure that the beneficiaries received their checks or that their families notify the Social Security Administration in Washington when the recipient dies.

Each of these foreign service officers reports to the ambassador on their programs, so the ambassador has the opportunity to take issue with a decision and disapprove it. At the same time, each FSO also reports to his/her Washington bureaucracy and thus receives two annual performance ratings: one from the ambassador and one from the FSO's Washington supervisor.

During the years I worked as an FSO, I was employed by the US Information Agency. We were known as USIA, referring to the Washington support operation, which was also the home offices and studios of the Voice of America (VOA). We and the rest of the world referred to our posts and personnel abroad as USIS, the U.S. Information Service. In some USIS posts, we had a resident American Voice of America correspondent. The VOA correspondent covered events in the country in which he resided, as well as neighboring countries, and his news reports to the Voice of America were not cleared by the ambassador.

Our responsibilities were generally two. We ran a local cultural program, which included the Fulbright Exchange program, lectures by well-known American speakers, and operated an American-style library. These libraries were frequently the most visible physical US presence in countries and therefore often became the target of unwelcome attention by local citizens unhappy with American foreign policy. Additionally, in those pre-Internet and pre-satellite broadcasting days, we offered current American films and produced performing arts programs, often in cooperation with local institutions.

We also invited local leaders as guests to the United States, giving them a firsthand look at our society and institutions. Interestingly, what seemed to impress many of these visitors most was the large number and efficiency of Americans who worked as volunteers in their local communities and the many national organizations with social or educational goals.

In addition to the cultural program, we had an information section, headed by an American FSO known as the information officer (IO). The IO was the embassy or consulate official spokesman and was in charge of both responding to media inquiries and getting stories placed in the local press or covered by local television stations. The IO also assisted visiting American journalists covering stories for major American media outlets.

USIS was run by a public affairs officer (PAO), assisted by a deputy PAO in the largest posts, as well as the information and cultural affairs officers. In the largest posts, they sometimes had FSO American assistants as well.

It was our collective job to know what I personally considered the most interesting people in the country to which we were assigned: educators, artists, intellectuals, and journalists who we hoped would be interested in the American point of view. Our motto became "Telling America's story to the world."

In addition to the American officers, we hired local citizens to keep us informed of the "movers and shakers" in the society we were charged with influencing. These Foreign Service National employees (FSNs) had difficult duties in sometimes difficult circumstances. American officers would come and go for two-, three-, or four-year tours; the FSNs had to bring each of them up to speed about who was who in the local culture.

Some American FSO supervisors were pleasant to work with; some were so taken with their own importance that they were deaf to good advice. I learned quickly that the FSNs were our first audience; if we couldn't convince them of our side of the story, how could we expect to influence the larger society? I learned to listen to them and was able to argue or question their recommended course of action. We had mutual respect for each other; some I still consider my closest friends, friendships kept alive by e-mail and telephone.

GREECE

CHAPTER 1

A Sioux in Greece

In May of 1968, I arrived in Athens as a US Information Agency (USIA) trainee. I was twenty-three years old. This was my first time crossing the Atlantic, not to mention proving myself in a new job. It was all a bit overwhelming, in spite of the fact that I'd done well in my six months of intensive Greek language and cultural training in Washington.

The post's courteous administrative officer met my wife and me at the airport, and, after retrieving our bags, we began the hour's trip through heavy traffic to our destination in the middle of the city. Even though I was tired after the all-night flight from Washington, DC, I was excited to be in the city for which I'd spent six months preparing. Sure enough, through the haze of Athens' air, I caught my first glimpse of the city's most famous landmark, the ancient Acropolis. The air, polluted by vehicle exhaust, obscured all but the most cursory impression of that famed fortress-like mountain in central Athens. We could barely make out the shape of Pericles' Parthenon, Athena's temple on top of the Acropolis, but it was enough to confirm that, like Dorothy in Oz, we weren't in Kansas anymore.

Our greeter showed us around the small temporary apartment where we would stay while looking for a house to rent and waiting for our meager household goods to make their

1

way by ship to Greece. After giving us a welcoming bottle of wine, he said goodbye, promising to pick me up at eight the next morning and take me to the office for my first day of work.

Sure enough, the car pulled up promptly the next morning, and he drove me to the office in a style to which I was definitely not accustomed. I was to begin my year of rotational training as the acting assistant cultural affairs officer, then move to the press and administrative sections, and even do a short stint with the public affairs officer as his staff assistant before spending a month or two in one of the embassy's sections: political, economic, commercial, or administrative.

Looking around my new office, I noticed that the in-box on my desk already had several papers and a file folder in it. This looked a bit intimidating since I had no idea what I was supposed to do with any piece of paper that came my way.

After a brief walk-through of our USIS offices and numerous introductory handshakes with the Greek employees from whom I would learn my job, I was taken to the embassy for the customary introductory call on the ambassador. As we walked through the halls, I noticed that instead of the usual institutional art on the walls, there was an interesting collection of paintings by what appeared to be Native Americans. But I had no opportunity to ask my escort why the dominant décor seemed to be primarily Indian. A few workmen were still opening crates in the hall and carefully removing paintings to be hung.

I remember little of meeting Ambassador Phillips Talbot except that he seemed uninterested in having to spend five minutes making conversation with a lowly trainee. The only thing that caught his attention was my Greek language training, noting that he approved of that. Talbot, a political appointee, was given no language training. While he wasn't likely to use the basic Greek he would have learned, he may have been mildly envious of those who had the opportunity to be less dependent on translators.

Returning to my office, I found that my immediate boss, the cultural attaché, was out, so I sat down at my desk and began to look at the papers in my in-box. Those in the file folder were relevant to my just-completed visit to the embassy: there was a memo from State, evidently responding to a request to Washington by Ambassador Talbot, asking for an exhibit of American art to display on embassy walls. Several other papers informed the ambassador that the only exhibit immediately available was a collection of American Indian art. It was obvious that the ambassador had accepted.

Four Greek women were working as cultural specialists in my office, and I approached one to see what she could tell me about the project. "Oh, the ambassador seemed intent on getting something truly American to decorate the embassy," she explained. "The only thing the State Department could come up with in a hurry was this group of paintings by *erithrodermi* (Indian) artists. I haven't even seen the paintings, but they must be interesting—after all, these Indians couldn't have much sense of art out there on their reservations."

I was surprised that I understood the word she used for Indian: "*erithrodhermi*," which literally translates to "redskins." It reminded me of something I'd learned during my Washington Greek studies: when faced with the need to invent a word, Greeks often took the English word apart and translated it literally. Since "Indian" in Greek means someone from India, that wouldn't do. Because most Greeks had seen enough American western movies to know the term "redskins," they collectively chose to translate "red" *(erethro)* and "skins" *(dhermi)* to refer to Native Americans.

What this translation missed was that these "redskins" were not whooping savages chasing western stagecoaches on horseback but, in fact, artists who had adopted sophisticated painting techniques and subjects that had caught the attention of the dominant white American culture. Of course, I too was ignorant of this: even though I had lived as a child in New Mexico close to a Mescalero Apache reservation, I had been completely unaware of the development of painting among our native population.

The point this sophisticated Greek woman was making without saying was that even though wonderful examples of American Indian art were hanging on embassy walls, in her opinion, there would be little interest among Greeks in seeing it as a public exhibition. To her, Indians were, after all, "primitives"; Greeks would hardly be interested in their artistic merits or lack thereof.

At that point, my supervisor returned to the office and welcomed me. "I see you've already been at your in-box," he said. "Good. I've got an idea about this Indian art."

The Greek woman with whom I had been speaking sniffed and walked away. I later learned that she had been a minority of one who thought this collection of paintings would be of no interest to Greeks. The other women in the office thought it would indeed be of interest but only in the less sophisticated provinces of Greece. So I'd picked up another bit of cultural information: many Athenian Greeks considered themselves the arbiters of artistic taste, more informed than their provincial compatriots. I'd already seen this in the United States: cosmopolitan East Coast Americans felt similarly about Montana or Kansas provincials knowing anything about "real" art.

My boss, Ted Wertime, was aware of this bias. In fact, when the file on Indian art had filtered down to him, he had deliberately saved it for my attention and action. He wouldn't try to change the Athenian bias, but he wanted to prove that folks in a provincial city would be interested in the chance to see something different. He explained to me later that in anticipation of my arrival, he had contacted our office's representative in Patras, a provincial capital in the southwest part of the Peloponnesian province, who had assured him that a public exhibition of Indian art would get an enthusiastic response.

"So," Ted concluded, "would you be willing to take the exhibit down to Patras and open it? I know you've just arrived and have only Washington Greek under your belt .... Oh! I almost forgot: we've arranged for the State Department to send us an American Indian artist to go along and be the center of attention, so you'd be his escort. Our man Demitri will set up the exhibit and send out invitations for a grand opening—he knows everyone in Patras. And since you're from Indian country, New Mexico, you would get along well with our Indian artist and be able to translate whatever he has to say to the guests."

I was (to put it mildly) floored. I hadn't even gotten to lunch on my first day at the office, and suddenly I was expected to be an authority on Indians, Indian art, and opening exhibitions—and to do it all in my newly minted but untested Greek.

Never one to doubt himself or others until they had proven themselves stupid, Ted took my astonished silence as consent. "Great," he boomed. "I knew you'd come through! The Indian artist is arriving early next week. His name is Oscar Howe, and he's famous for having decorated the Corn Palace in South Dakota. Your wife can stay here in Athens to look for a house to rent; we'll send you to the airport to pick up the artist and leave directly for Patras, where Demitri will have everything ready. You'll only be gone a couple of nights."

Heretofore, I'd simply stood with an astonished look, but I finally found my tongue. "Ted, I don't know a damned thing about Indian art—in fact, any kind of art! Just being born in New Mexico doesn't mean I know anything about Indians. They were all on the reservation, and I was just a kid when we moved to Texas. And with only six months of intensive but basic Greek under my belt, I can't expect to use it to explain a subject I know nothing about!"

"Grimland, you worry too much! Get our American library to pull together some material on Indian art. They have a great research capability over there. Brush up on your Greek for anything you didn't learn in Washington, and find out whatever you need to know about Oscar Howe and the Corn Palace in South Dakota. You've got a whole week to prepare." The Internet and Wikipedia had not been invented in 1968, but Ted believed religiously in the wonders of old-fashioned libraries and people who knew how to use them. In the face of Ted's confidence and enthusiasm, the only thing I could mutter was, "Yes, sir."

The next week was hell. I remember lugging home heavy piles of reference books on the bus (my ride to work that first morning had been a one-time favor), reading well into the night until I fell asleep and showing up bleary-eyed at the office the next day to soak in as much as I could from brief State Department bio sketches of the Sioux artist, Oscar Howe.

Even though panicked, I was interested. Howe, a Yankton Sioux, was honored as the American Indian painter who had introduced abstractionism to Indian art, combining it with traditional Indian style to develop a new school of artistic expression. Being chosen to decorate the Corn Palace in Mitchell, South Dakota seemed a minor honor compared to his other contributions to art. But I would learn in later conversations with him that he considered his work at the Corn Palace an important milestone in his career.

More daunting than the stacks of library books, however, was the challenge of trying in a few days to learn how to express all this art history of a different culture in Greek. My success was to prove mixed.

The days passed quickly, and I had barely recovered from jet lag when I found myself in a car headed for the airport to pick up Howe and go directly to Patras. The road from Athens to Patras heads south across the Corinth Canal and then turns west to bypass the modern city of Corinth, cutting across the northern Peloponnesus to Patras, just to the south of where the Gulf of Corinth meets the Ionian Sea. It was Greece's third largest urban area after Athens and Thessaloniki.

As we traveled, I tried to act as tour guide for Howe; I had learned as part of my Greek studies some of the important geographic and ancient sites of central Greece but was seeing them now for the first time myself. We stopped at the Corinth Canal, treated ourselves to a snack of small kebabs on wooden sticks, then walked over to view the canal from a bridge some two hundred feet above it and marveled at the nineteenth century engineering that had cut this channel almost vertically through limestone.

As we drove around the modern city of Corinth, I could see the ancient acropolis of the city, fortified first by the Greeks, then by Norman Crusader armies, and finally by the Venetians. Howe was silent through most of my occasionally informed patter but perked up when I mentioned the Crusader fortifications.

"You mean the Crusaders who were led by King Arthur?" he asked.

"Uh, no, sir, the Crusades passed through here in 1204, long after King Arthur in Britain died and became the premier myth of Western culture."

Howe paused thoughtfully. "I don't know about the Crusades you're talking about. I thought that all that stuff about Crusades referred to King Arthur's time. And now you're telling me he is a myth. I'm sorry; I didn't get much history in Indian schools."

I felt badly for embarrassing him. "Well, sir, I don't know much about American Indian art, but I'm sure learning fast."

Howe smiled. "I don't know much about it either," he said. "When I was a kid we were pretty poor, and to make matters worse, I contracted some kind of eye disease and was almost blind. I was so discouraged. I'd never have been able to go to school if my tribe hadn't had a tradition every year of giving a pony to a poor member of the tribe who was sick. I guess they figured it would help give him some hope, something to live for. And one year I was the one they gave the pony to."

I'm not often at a loss for words, but I didn't know what to say. So for a few long moments, I unintentionally did the right thing and said nothing. Finally, and I wasn't being dramatic, I sighed heavily and said, "That *was* powerful, Mr. Howe. I hope I'm never in your position ... because I don't have a tribe that understands."

"Yes ... and call me Oscar, ... Dave."

A couple of hours later, we came to the outskirts of Patras. I'd been told our office was downtown, which was easy to find in those days.

"I have to admit, Oscar, I don't know the drill on what happens when we get there. I've never even met our representative down here. So we'll wing it, okay?" Oscar agreed, and I felt nervous that he had put himself in my hands.

At our office, a large crowd of people blocked the street, and a circle of local dignitaries stood by the door with a red, white, and blue ribbon strung across it. A neatly dressed man with a large pair of scissors seemed to stand out. I got out of the car first, Oscar sliding over to exit behind me.

"*Kyrie Demitri?*" (Mr. Demitri) I said before taking refuge in English. "I'm David Grimland ... and this is our honored guest, Mr. Oscar Howe."

Demitri, who was middle-aged and therefore older than I, looked pleased that I'd used "*Kyrie*," the honorific comparable to "Mr.," and shook hands with us both. "Let me first introduce you and Mr. Howe to our dignitaries ... in order of rank," he whispered. "Only a few of them speak any English. If you need help, I'm right behind you."

We proceeded to the dozen or so Greeks waiting near the ribbon: the mayor, the police chief, local military commanders, and their wives. In my classroom Greek, I managed the correct comments of being glad or honored to meet them and immediately introduced Oscar as "our honored guest," noting his fame as an American Indian artist. As we got to the ribbon, Demitri made a short speech welcoming everyone and introducing Mr. Howe, *O perifimos erethrodermos kalitexnis* ("the famous Indian artist") who would cut the ribbon himself. He handed the scissors to Oscar, who knew what he was supposed to do. Before cutting it, he made a few impromptu remarks about being honored to open this exhibit in the beautiful city of Patras. Demitri translated his remarks into Greek for the crowd. (I wasn't willing to be too extemporaneous at that point.)

With a snip it was done, and Oscar and I walked into a beautifully arranged exhibit of a dozen of the paintings I'd last seen going up on the embassy wall in Athens. This time they were set up on easels for closer viewing. The dignitaries followed us, a small knot of obviously important citizens behind them. We came to the first painting. It was, even to my artistically blind eye, several stalks of American corn in a field, the sun shining from one side of the canvas and rainclouds gathering on the other.

The little knot of people had grown to two or three people deep, as guests crowded forward to see the painting and even more for a close-up look at the first real American Indian they'd ever seen. A senior military officer, evidently claiming his right to speak first, looked at the painting and said, in Greek, "Please ask our honored guest to tell us what this painting means." I translated for Oscar.

Oscar looked thoughtfully at the painting for a few moments and said quietly to me, "I have no idea what this means; this is a Navajo painting—I'm a Sioux."

I remember feeling only a moment of panic. "Well," I said to Oscar in a whisper: "Could you please say something, anything, about the images you see?" He looked puzzled but complied. I turned to the dignitaries and said in Greek (I think):

"Mr. Howe says this is a field of corn. It is fed by Father Sun on the left and watered by Mother Rain on the right. Corn is sacred to the American Indians and represents the cycle of life upon which we all depend." I was guessing, of course, but based on my hurried research of the previous week it seemed like a pretty good guess.

I wondered whether I'd gotten all the words correct, but then I heard murmurs of understanding and agreement. We moved to the second painting. Again my uneducated eye saw a hillside with American bison grazing and Indian hunters creeping up through the tall grass toward them.

Again: "Please ask our honored guest what this painting means." Oscar's reply: "I think this is a Plains Indian painting. I'm a Sioux and I can't be sure of what the artist is telling us." Again, I murmured, "Could you say just enough to make it sound like you know? I'll try to make up the rest." Smiling ever so slightly, Oscar now caught on to the game and complied. I listened and nodded, then turned to the group and said in Greek:

"Mr. Howe says that the buffalo are the heart and soul of the Indians who live on the plains. The buffalo provide meat and hides; even the bones are roasted to provide nourishing food and feed the women and children. The hunters are lying in the grass asking the Great Father for success in the hunt, which is about to start."

More appreciative murmurs, but I wondered how long my vocabulary was going to be adequate to the task.

And so it went with the third, fourth, and fifth paintings— not one Sioux work of art among them. I worked to keep from getting too far from the words I knew, several times pausing to publicly ask Demitri how to say something in Greek. But we hit a deadly snag on the last painting, which showed a tepee with warriors dancing near it and a pole with painted scalps moving slightly in a painted breeze.

I had no idea what "scalp" was in Greek and neither did Demitri. So I explained that it was "cutting the hair off the head, sort of like a 'haircut.'"

Some consternation was apparent among our guests. "Doesn't that hurt?" someone asked. "Yes," I replied, "but it was not always fatal. The number of scalps a warrior takes is a sign of his bravery and warrior skill."

By that time, we'd reached the end of the displayed paintings, and glasses of wine with little hors d'oeuvres filled a table. Fortunately, the crowd broke into conversational knots with simple patter I could handle alone, while Demitri fielded questions to Oscar and relayed his replies. I could get the drift of what Oscar was saying and learned something that I would use throughout my entire foreign service career.

When the questioning got deeper than Oscar could handle, he merely changed the subject and asked the Greeks something about what he had seen on his trip as we entered Patras—a large church, a part of a fortress wall. Nothing deflects a questioner like the opportunity to talk proudly about his home turf and impress the guest with information about something of which he is knowledgeable. Oscar was then free to respond knowledgeably about what it was like to grow up as a poor American Indian, struggling to get an education. He wasn't expected to be an expert on the sights of Patras, and he was admired for admitting he didn't know and for appreciating what he was told. He became a "real" person, still somewhat exotic but showing signs of humanity that many Greeks could understand.

I have no idea how many hearts and minds we affected that evening. For some years I worried about my little deceptions in making up things that Oscar supposedly said about the paintings. I finally forgave myself by realizing that I'd done no more than spare Oscar and the American flag the embarrassment of not knowing what was in our own exhibit. By passing on my limited knowledge in their own language I offered a compliment to them and a relief for Oscar and myself. There are, after all, worse sins in the practice of public diplomacy.

We must have spent the night in Patras; I simply do not remember. But the next day we returned to Athens, again via the modern and classical cities of Corinth. I took time out to have the driver take us up to the top of the ancient acropolis just outside the modern town and was able to point out the icon of St. Mark carved into the outermost defensive walls and, a little higher up the hill, the crumbling stonework thrown up hastily as the Norman Crusaders passed through in 1204 on their way to sack the city of Constantinople in what is now Turkey. All this expertise was courtesy of Fodor's *Guide to Greece*, which I had purchased on my second day in the country.

During the ride home, Oscar spoke a little about how proud he was of having been invited to decorate the Corn Palace in Mitchell. Indeed, he learned something about ancient and modern Greek history, and I learned even more about at least one Indian. We were both a little wiser.

At the end of the Patras trip, I delivered Oscar to Ambassador Talbot in Athens, where Oscar kindly sang my praises as a Greek translator and "quick thinker." Our respect for each other was genuine, and we shook hands with special warmth when I took him to the airport for his return journey to the Dakotas, which he had represented so well in Greece.

Oscar Howe was the first of many American visitors to my foreign service posts who, over the years, gave me a unique opportunity to *listen* and learn. I count few American politicians in that category, but the visiting educators, artists, even the young sailors whose ships happened to be in port and who ended up at our home for Thanksgiving or Christmas dinner. Too often we assume that our professional contacts in a country of assignment are the only sources of learning. Many of them were. The men and women in Greece or Turkey or India or Bangladesh or Cyprus whom I grew to know in the course of work certainly played helpful roles in my understanding and appreciation of their countries as well as my own. But those whom fate washed up on my shores were also part of the mix. All played a part in creating the strangely beautiful tapestry we later call education that might lead someday to wisdom.

> *"Education is a progressive discovery*
> *of our own ignorance."*
> Will Durant

CHAPTER 2

Relevance of Strabo Today

Soon after I arrived in Athens in 1968, I was assigned a Greek tutor to bring my spoken Greek up to useful speed. Even after six months of intensive language training in Washington, DC, it was difficult, if not impossible, to really speak any foreign language based on classroom instruction alone.

Evdhoxia was a young woman studying archaeology and thus had learned some classical Greek. She later went on to be a professor of history at a women's college in Athens founded by Americans in the nineteenth century and has published two historical novels.

She taught me modern Greek, but I still remember her teaching me one classical Greek saying, telling me that I would occasionally hear it from educated Greeks—and in the ancient Greek in which it was first written:

Ou pandos plein eis tin Korinthon.

Not everyone can go to Corinth.

This was written by Strabo (64 BC to 24 AD) from his work entitled *Geography*. Strabo was a wealthy, well-traveled Greek philosopher who lived in the Roman-conquered Greek colony of Pontos, now northern Turkey, near the Black Sea.

His expression recalls the actual history of visiting the Greek city of Corinth at the time. About one thousand *hetaeras* (courtesans) served in the temple of Aphrodite, the goddess of love. *Hetaeras* in classical Greece were highly educated, sophisticated companions, and although most engaged in sexual relations with their patrons, *hetaeras* were not common temple prostitutes.

The *hetaeras* serving Aphrodite were said to be the most beautiful, talented, and expensive. Thus "going to Corinth" and enjoying the company of these women was not something the poor or even the middle class in classical Greece could ever hope to afford. These women often grew wealthy on their cut of the donations given by rich patrons for the upkeep of the temple and by the connections they made with patrons and donors. They also profited from a little business on the side. A famous Greek actually married a *hetaera* he met in the course of donating to a major temple. When they married he learned that her income was higher than his and permitted (insisted?) that she continue her occupation, at least until he decided he was ready to father children.

Strabo's expression obviously means that only the wealthy can afford the good things of life. Seems very appropriate two thousand years later.

CHAPTER 3

Koutouki

Koutouki has now come to imply "fashionable" and therefore "good." But the best places to eat in Athens in the late 1960s were introduced to me before they became fashionable. Then *koutouki* just meant good, cheap food and plenty of wine straight from the barrel. The eateries were small: the Greek word *koutouki* literally means "little box." My wife and I could eat a great meal for fifty *drachmas*—about a dollar and fifty cents at the time.

I was first taken to a *koutouki* by a group of young Greek artists and intellectuals whom I had gotten to know during my first year in Athens. I was the embassy "youth officer," and it was part of my job to meet and know the younger leftist-inclined painters, poets, novelists—anyone creative and careful enough to escape the unwelcome attention of the Greek junta that took over Greece in 1967 in the name of making the country a "Greece of Greeks and Christians" *(Ellas, Ellinon, Xristianon!)*.

I remember when I first arrived in Athens and was told that I, still a trainee in the United States Information Agency, was to be accorded the questionable honor of being the embassy's "youth officer." I asked my boss, the embassy's cultural attaché, why, just because I was young myself, I was qualified to know anything about younger Greeks. I had no interest in being typecast in a particular role. "Hell, Grimland," my boss thundered. "Just because you act as though you were born thirty years old doesn't mean you've forgotten how to relate to younger Greeks. Now get out there and meet some!"

I don't remember that this *koutouki* had a name—it was simply called "Panayotis' Place" (the owner/cook's name). It was down the hill south of the Hilton Hotel in a truly working-class neighborhood; the residents of the area were laborers and lower-middle-class folks. I don't know whether Panayiotis' Place survived being discovered by artists, but during my three years there, it served good food and offered, importantly for me, a glimpse of Greek life I couldn't have gotten at fancier eating places.

The atmosphere of the place was authentic: no fancy tablecloths, no silver cutlery, or crystal glassware. Instead, a jukebox near the door blared arabesque music, and real working men frequented the place. Panayiotis' was small: the eating area had perhaps four heavy wooden tables squeezed in along each of two walls, separated by an aisle of perhaps three feet. A heavy timber rack over one of the rows of tables held six huge wooden barrels of table wine, all of it the *retsina* favored by folks with little concern about wine except it's quantity and price. I'd gotten to like the stuff. It was flavored with pine pitch ("resin" -- thus *retsina*), and it went well with a heavy olive-oil-based cuisine.

All the cooking was done by Panayotis and his wife in a tiny kitchen that looked like it would do fine as a submarine galley. It was served by his plump ten-year-old daughter, and came in hot and cold courses like appetizers. There were small dishes of home-cured olives, feta cheese, some salty cheddar-like cheese, fresh sardines (whole, small fish that had never seen a can) fried in olive oil and served with large wedges of fresh Cretan lemons, tiny peeled shrimp, a water glass containing crisp Romaine lettuce leaves in lemon juice, and, of course, baskets of fresh bread.

The first course of appetizers was followed by small plates of fried *calamari,* grilled liver dusted in spicy flour, and/or small shish kebabs heavily flavored with thyme from the flanks of Mount Hymitos on the eastern edge of the city. Dessert was a large plate of whatever fruit was in season (which meant almost every kind, since most of it came from Crete's warmer climate far to the south of the mainland).

While my new leftist friends soon tired of Panayiotis' and moved on to discover a new "workers" eatery, I continued to patronize the restaurant, coming with my wife and even bringing her mother and sister when they visited. This was unusual, since I never saw another female customer in the place.

When I first started coming to the *koutouki*, I'd had only my Washington-based Greek language training. My Greek was passable but overly formal for the setting and working -class clientele, and my speaking attempts were often greeted by humorous but helpful comments from the other customers who spoke a rapid "villager" dialect (compared to the grammatically correct "diplomatic" Greek I'd learned in Washington.) One couldn't have asked for a better language and cultural learning environment: good food lubricated by good wine and interesting company.

I remember vividly two incidents at Panayiotis' Place, both humorous with tragic overtones. The first involved a local customer confined to a wheelchair. He would roll his chair up to the door and bang on the window with his cane. A couple of patrons would get up and carry him in to sit with them. I don't remember his name, but whenever I saw him, I would send over a glass of *retsina* (drawn from the barrel of choice above our heads) or a plate of especially good fruit and cheese. He would graciously raise his glass to me and I to him, and others would join in the toast with short, flowery speeches. This was a culturally accepted way for me to become "one of the boys."

One night, he (I'll call him "Georgos") was seated at his table, sipping his wine and nibbling on the fresh, delicious food, when suddenly from outside a loud crash signaled an accident. Everyone rushed outside except Georgos who sat shouting to be brought out.

It was a dismal scene. A car coming up the darkened street (no street lights in this poor part of town) had hit the wheelchair. It lay on the ground, one of the wheels knocked off and part of the frame bent. The driver of the car had stopped briefly, thrown some money at the chair, and raced away.

The customers, joined now by Georgos, examined the damage, loudly cursing the absent driver. After the requisite shouting, some of them disappeared to their scooters or scooter-trucks and came back with tools. They began to bang on the wheelchair, trying to get it back in shape.

Muttering to himself and anyone who listened, Georgos alternately bemoaned his fate and shouted instructions and curses at the repair team. Somehow, in less than a half-hour's wrangling and shouting, they managed to get the wheel back on and the frame reasonably straightened out. Someone less mechanically inclined had already gone around in the dark collecting the coins the driver had flung out, and brought them back to Georgos.

Finally, Georgos was lifted into the chair. He took a few turns around the street, smiled broadly, and pronounced it as good as new. So he was again lifted up and taken back into the *koutouki*, where everyone followed and liberally treated themselves to liquid congratulations on their expertise.

After a couple of hours of drinking and eating, Georgos was unsteadily lifted back into his chair and weaved off down the street into the night. For some reason, it was both a humorous and heartwarming night—one that still brings back a gentle smile as I remember it.

The other evening that resonates in my memory was the night my wife and I took Jackie (a visiting American secretary at our office) to the restaurant. Jackie was classically gorgeous: a blue-eyed blonde with a perfect complexion and engaging smile. One of the young workers who was a regular customer—I remember his name was Stavros—immediately fell in love with her. Greeks go nuts over blonde foreigners, assuming (incorrectly) that all the ancient Greeks had flowing yellow locks. Stavros' distinguishing badge of honor was that he had a wooden hand (the original was lost in some industrial accident).

As the evening wore on, Stavros kept ordering plates of fruit or other delicacies to send to our beautiful guest while he succeeded in working himself up into a *retsina*-induced frenzy. Even though I kept sending small carafes of *retsina* and small plates of food back to even the hospitality contest, it seemed only to further fan the fires of Stavros' passion.

He finally got up and came weaving over (about four steps) to our table. He was so drunk he could hardly stand but stood there braying like a donkey and singing along with whatever mournful song was coming out of the jukebox. At one point, obviously to impress Jackie, he grabbed a heavy wooden table loaded with dishes and picked it up with his one good hand, Panayiotis hovering nearby to prevent any of the plates or glasses from sliding off.

He finally declared that she (and my wife and I as her chaperones) had to come home and meet his mother. It didn't take a genius to figure out that this was getting serious, and I began to ponder a way to get us out of a delicate situation. But for now he insisted vehemently that Jackie had to come meet "Mama." It was after midnight by this time, and all the other customers were enjoying the show and unhelpfully egging on our increasingly drunk lover.

So after paying our bill, Stavros, Jackie, and I walked about two doors away and woke up Mama. The young man explained to her that he was going to ask Jackie to marry him, at which point he collapsed on his mother's couch and passed out. His mother looked at me, at beautiful Jackie, and said *"Ti na kano? Pandote, eine to idho me ton Stavro. Ti boro na po?"* ("What can I do? It's always the same with Stavros. What can I say to him?")

In a flash of impromptu genius, I responded, *"Pes ton Stavro oti Jackie then eine Orthodoxos— eine Protestantis, kai then bori na eine mia 'kali' yeneka yia ton Stavro."* ("Tell Stavros that Jackie isn't an Orthodox Christian, and therefore she cannot be a proper wife for him.")

Fortunately, by that time Stavros was oblivious even to Jackie's charms. *"Kala,"* ("Good") his mother said. *"Efxaristo. Tha tu po avrio. Efxaristo!-- ise kalos -- oxi -- sophos -- agori -- oxi -- andros! Kali nixta sas, kai efharisto!* ("Good night and thank you! You are a good boy—no—a wise man. Good night.") And she smiled sadly as we walked out into the night.

I've wondered over the years since, how Stavros took the news the next morning. Somehow I hope he sobered up and bought the *Orthodoxia* excuse I had invented on the spot. It would have made good cultural sense, but where love (or lust) is concerned, religious doctrine usually takes a back seat.

I've always remembered Jackie and Stavros—and Stavros' kind mother. To be twenty-four years old, and called a "wise man." ... well, it may have been overstated, but it was—and remains—very touching.

CHAPTER 4

Of Monks and Lobsters

I don't remember how long I'd been working in Athens, but I had fallen back into the habit of going to the American Ecumenical Church without much feeling or thought about either the ceremony or the theology but still involving myself as choir director and eventual president of the congregation.

However, the minister was probably the most interesting aspect of the whole experience.

Otto Meinardus had been a Nazi soldier in the Second World War. Wounded on the Russian front, he'd been pulled out of the freezing snow by Russian peasants. For some reason, they had nursed him back to health and turned him over to a smuggling gang that had somehow gotten him out of the country. He ended up in the United States, where he entered seminary and became a minister.

As a result of his miraculous chance at a second life, he studied the (seemingly, to us) arcane minutia of early Christianity and sought out ecumenical churches serving the expatriate community in places such as Athens. The congregations were not large, nor were his prospects for advancement, but Otto offered something quite unexpected, not just to his parish flock but to the generally unchurched diplomatic crowd. He was eager to share his knowledge of the unusual.

Mount Athos, in northern Greece, certainly qualified as unusual. It lies just to the southeast of Thessaloniki, where a large peninsula called Chalkidiki hangs down from the Greek mainland; off the large peninsula are another three smaller finger-like peninsulas, stretching some fifty kilometers into the Aegean Sea. The easternmost peninsula is labeled Athos. This peninsula is largely a mountain for its entire length, with some twenty or so Greek, Russian, and Serbian monasteries.

Mount Athos is part of Greece but is ruled by the monasteries. The Greek government controls its foreign affairs, provides some emergency services such as fire and medical evacuation, and issues visas to visitors.

Perhaps most interesting, Athos's rule strictly prevents women from coming to the monasteries, even setting foot on the peninsula, whether they are pilgrims or sightseers. Female journalists regularly tried to dress and act like males, and all who were found out were quickly deported.

Otto had gotten the word around and gathered a group of men from the American Embassy in Athens for a four-day visit to some of the more famous monasteries during the last week of Lent. We were warned that the meals would be increasingly restricted during the days we were there; meat was off the list, and by the end of our visit even olive oil would not be available. Beans or lentils, rice, bread, and monastery wine would be served, but Otto encouraged us travelers to fill our small packs with tinned sardines, sausages, and plenty of fruit bars.

About a dozen of us signed up. We took a plane from Athens to Thessaloniki, then traveled by bus to the edge of Chalkidiki, where we met a chartered fishing boat that took us by sea around the Athos peninsula and dropped us off at the docks of the most well-known monasteries.

Why were we interested in visiting? The monasteries on Athos are veritable storehouses of historical treasures: famous icons, illustrated manuscripts, libraries of correspondence, and legal documents dating back to the monasteries' founding in the ninth to eleventh centuries. Often on parchment scrolls, the documents are stored in small cabinets as they were in ancient time.

Visits invariably followed the same routine. We all traipsed up to the crenellated walls. (The monasteries in past centuries had been repeatedly attacked by pirates, who were after the gold and silver religious items—candlesticks, ceremonial plates, ornately carved metal cups, precious icons—as well as documents of antiquarian value which could be sold all over the Mediterranean.)

Once we had been admitted through massive wooden gates reinforced with metal bands, we were taken to the guest reception room, where the monks served glasses of water each with a spoon of sticky sweet jam, a glass of ouzo, and then Turkish-style coffee. The guest master or often the abbot would greet us in one or more modern languages. They were always pleased to learn that a number of us spoke decent Greek. Even though the monks spoke Greek, Russian, or Serbian, the language of commerce with fishermen or farmers bringing sheep and goats for sale would be Greek, and that was the *lingua franca* of the Holy Mountain.

Monks worked the monastery vegetable gardens, but there were plenty of acolytes to do the heavy lifting. Most of the monks were not priests but rather lay brothers who had retired to the monastery after their wives died.

We stopped first at the Russian orthodox monastery, Pantelemonon. Vladimir Putin would visit about thirty years later, in 1998. But at the time we went there, Russian governmental interest had been limited to keeping thirty to forty monks supplied to ensure Pantelemonon's seat on the governing council of Athos, which was composed of representatives from all the viable institutions.

I remember eating in its refectory one of our few filling meals of lentils and rice, cooked in a copper cauldron perhaps four feet in diameter and ten inches deep. (When not in use as a cooking pot, it was used to wash clothes. No one asked whether it would have been declared "clean" between washing and cooking.) The refectory was decorated with scenes of hell: fierce monsters vividly chewing on squirming sinners or roasting them over eternal fires. Well ... it did whet the appetite for lentils and rice....

We gradually worked our way by boat from the northwestern coast, around the southern tip of the Athos peninsula and north up the eastern coast. As we rounded the southern tip of Athos, one of the spring storms that bring rain for the crops blew in, and the sea turned to a heaving mass of choppy waves, resulting in some serious seasickness among those prey to it and soaking all of us in a cold, windy rain.

We couldn't help but remember that the Persian King Darius, in the fifth century BCE, had lost three hundred ships carrying an army and supplies with which he intended to invade Greece. That invasion was scrapped, of course, but Darius' son Xerxes was more successful.

Xerxes cut a channel for his ships across the isthmus. He later made an unenviable reputation at a famous mountain pass in southern Greece named *Thermopylae* (see Notes for more background on *Thermopylae*), before attacking Athens in the south of Greece. But the fate of Darius' ships was on our minds as we pitched in the cold waves and rain.

Our last visit was to the largest of the Greek monasteries, Stavronikiti, named (by tradition) after two mythically famous monks in the tenth century, Stavros and Nikos, and dedicated to St. Nikolas. We arrived late at Stavronikiti and were shown immediately to the refectory. The guest master apologized that the monks were all at vespers and would have their humble supper after services (around midnight). Since this was the end of Lent, he could offer us only some beans and torn-up lettuce leaves—no olive oil or vinegar—just "naked" lettuce. We all somberly assured him that we understood that we were remembering Christ's passion and would be content with our simple fare.

As soon as we finished dinner, we were shown to our cells and immediately dug into our packs to dine on cans of sardines, tuna fish, and hidden saltines. Not great but better than dry lettuce and beans; we hoped Christ would understand.

The next morning I awoke earlier than usual and, not having bathed or shaved for three days, took my razor to the kitchen hoping to find a pan and warm up some shaving water on the wood stove.

I beat the cook into the kitchen and noticed on one side our unwashed plates from the night before piled up near the large marble sink with a few shreds of lettuce and some beans that had escaped someone's spoon. On the other side of the sink, however, were the remains of the monks' "simple" repast. No lettuce and beans: instead the crockery was piled high with empty lobster shells and what looked suspiciously like butter sauce.

I shaved and returned to our rooms, shaking Otto awake to ask him why the double-dining standard.

Otto chuckled and explained that the prohibition on meat or even fish did not apply since the lobster's blood was not red but green. And butter was permissible because it was "modern" and rarely eaten. Olive oil was likely specifically mentioned in the ancient documents as prohibited. Butter would likely not have been known in medieval Greece. The quantity of milk needed for butter would not have been available from the poorly fed cows of the day nor would the butter have kept without refrigeration. Thus the monks were within their literal rights to have butter sauce on their bloodless lobsters.

While one had to admire the clever negotiation around the literal prohibition on pleasure in a time of remembering the Christ's passion, we could only wish that the good monks had shared their pleasure with us, in the name of Christian charity. However, since the monks correctly surmised that we were either Protestants or, worse, Roman Catholics, they felt no need to share their secret. Orthodox Eastern Christians considered both as theologically and historically untrustworthy.

Our time was up the next day, so after matins we stuffed our dirty clothes in our packs, put on our last clean underwear and socks, and made our way down to our boat, hoping against hope that the captain hadn't had enough of us and would be there. Someone voiced his concern to Otto, and Otto, chuckling, said, "You don't think I paid him more than a minimum before we left, do you? He'll be there."

CHAPTER 5

The Holy Land: Church, Politics … and Tradition

Note: I have included this story under the Greece section because I was assigned to Greece at the time we made this visit to the Holy Land.

It is important to be aware of and reflect on the complexity of Holy Land church politics, a centuries-old mix of money, custom, religion, and tradition that always underlies Middle Eastern issues. For example, the United Nations Organization for Education, Science, and Culture (UNESCO) is reported to be working on getting the Church of the Nativity in Bethlehem designated as a World Heritage Site. The Palestinian political leadership supports this effort; they welcome any way they could get world attention leading to recognition for Palestine as a state. Greek Orthodox leaders, however, are uneasy with UNESCO or secular Palestinian involvement in the status of the Bethlehem church; their traditional control of all matters concerning this church might be threatened by secular political meddling.

Church versus secular control aside, a bewildering variety of mainly Eastern Christian denominations control the major Christian sites in Jerusalem and the surrounding area. Whole churches or various parts of the sanctuaries are owned by different denominations: Armenian, Russian Orthodox, Syrian, Syrian Orthodox, Marionite, and Egyptian Coptic.

Churches in Eastern Christianity are very much concerned with who controls what at their numerous pilgrimage sites. Control is based on a long history of how each site was acquired, how valuable it is—meaning how many pilgrims visit the site and leave contributions, the ability of the mother church to support the physical upkeep and personnel to lure pilgrims, and a long list of factors that emerge from any corporate bureaucracy.

The division of religious sites is easy to observe in a visit to the Church of the Holy Sepulcher in Jerusalem (a rambling structure covering several traditional sites: the prison where Jesus was held and scourged; Golgotha, where he was crucified; and the tomb where his body lay for three days until the Resurrection). Several sects own the rights to these sites: the Greek Orthodox own Golgotha and the tomb as well as several lesser-known sites; Armenians own the prison of Jesus; the Franciscans the place where he was whipped; the Syrian Orthodox own a little piece of the rock that formed the tomb and so on.

Whether these sites are historically accurate is irrelevant; they have been steeped in the prayers of centuries of pilgrims and are accepted by the faithful as true. Pilgrims from wealthy Americans to Palestinian laborers come on major festival dates such as Christmas and Easter but also on lesser dates set aside by scholars or tradition to pray, light candles, and leave considerable offerings.

All of these sites have been bought and paid for by the wealthier mother churches. Many of them, particularly the

Greek Orthodox, get this money from their monasteries in Greece. There are even Greek monasteries in other parts of the Middle East that get huge numbers of Christian pilgrims, and part of the proceeds goes toward upkeep and support of the priests at the Church of the Holy Sepulcher. Other income is available because some monasteries are allowed to own commercial or agricultural land and collect the rents. For example, the Greek monasteries on Mount Athos in northern Greece own prime shopping properties. So when the Greek patriarch needs a little spending money to buy another scrap of a particularly lucrative pilgrim site, he taps the monasteries and Greek churches in faraway lands, and he gets the funds.

The wealthiest monastery in Cyprus bought a submarine for the Greek navy, and in the spring of 2013, when Cyprus was having its banking crisis, the Cypriot Orthodox Church announced that it would float a loan to save the Cypriot economy. One of the Cypriot Church's tenants is the new American Embassy in Cyprus, built on what was a beautiful olive orchard in what used to be the outskirts of the capital, Nicosia. The embassy contractors had to cut down a number of olive trees, some very ancient and still producing good fruit, in order to open up visual security spaces.

The churches guard their traditional prerogatives zealously. I learned much of this in three visits to the "holy land" in the late 1960s and early 1970s. My first trip was as a member of the Ecumenical Protestant Church in Athens. The minister of the church was Rev. Otto Meinardus, a German whom the reader met in the preceding chapter.

Otto's research specialty was in first century BCE Christianity, and so he ended up being an expert on the history and development of holy sites in Egypt, Palestine, Israel, Syria, Cyprus, and Armenia. In the process, he got to know the churches and the individual monks and priests who were assigned to watch over their properties and collect donations.

Thus it was Otto who arranged with the monks of the Church of the Holy Sepulcher for our little band of pilgrims to spend most of the night in the church. It is usually locked from sunset to sunrise. By tradition, the key to the church is in the possession of an old Ottoman Muslim family, but the huge iron lock on the front door hangs far above the height of a man. The only ladder that may be used to climb up to the lock is held by the monks inside the church; they open a small hatch in the massive wooden door every evening to push the ladder, practically a relic itself, out to the man waiting with the key.

He comes twice a day: at daybreak he returns to climb up and unlock the door to allow the day's visitors to come in; in the evening, he climbs up and locks it to prevent visitors or thieves from getting in. We not only witnessed this tradition but, once locked inside for the night, we got a glimpse of the elaborate procedures that the monks went through in checking all their properties and making sure nothing was amiss. With very few exceptions, little of the modern world disturbs these centuries-old traditions. The same routine controls the lives of those inside: they eat the same meals on the same days; they pray the same prayers at the same times and places; and they are always present when visitors are around.

Watching the ceremonial routines was fascinating. Tradition demands that a representative of each sect owning a site cense and bless the site every night of the year beginning precisely at midnight and ending within a certain time. And the kicker is that only one individual could do the censing in a night— no relays, no passing of the baton, or censor in this case, is permitted. This wasn't a problem for the sects that owned one or two sites in close proximity, but the Greeks had so many significant properties spread out all over the huge, rambling building that it required a highly trained priest in excellent physical condition to scamper around waving his censor and muttering, "In-the-name-of-the-Father-Son-and-Holy-Ghost" as he ran past. Representatives of the other sects were hovering nearby, because if the Greek runner missed one of the sites or made a mistake in the wording or if his censor had gone out, the first onlooker could jump out and bless the site, and it would be his sect's forever.

We watched with interest as a young Greek priest came up to the starting point. With an acolyte helping him, he removed his black oxfords and put on a pair of Nike running shoes. He stripped off his long black outer robe, and then tucked the end of his shorter blue under-robe up and over his belt. After checking his censor, he waited tensely for the stroke from a large clock, which signaled midnight. We held our breaths as the seconds ticked away.

The first stroke bonged, and the Greek shot off like a sprinter at a track meet, waving his censor at each Greek site and simultaneously muttering the magic words of blessing, then continuing on to the next. It took about twenty-five minutes for him to cover his stops.

Otto, who was giving us a running commentary on the proceedings, told us that the sects historically have used less peaceful means to protect their properties. According to him:

> There was a fourth man who died on Calvary where Jesus and the two thieves were crucified. In the nineteenth century, an unknown "troublemaker" tried to put a sign on the little mound saying "Golgotha belongs to ALL." He was shot dead by a Greek monk guarding the mound. No investigation was conducted by the local political authorities (likely the Ottoman governor of Jerusalem); no unclaimed body was ever discovered. The senior Greek cleric inside the church simply relied on his traditional (and accepted) authority to take care of the problem.

That night in the Church of the Holy Sepulcher, I thought of that fourth man who died on Calvary trying to express a powerful truth by holding up his crude, hand-lettered sign. Golgotha does indeed belong to all!

By the end of the week, we dozen pilgrims had pretty much had it with seeing the many holy sites, walking the Via Dolorosa, sitting around the pool of Bethesda, or driving to Nazareth to see an unremarkable modern Catholic church commemorating where Jesus spent his boyhood. After all, one can take just so much holiness. But on our last day in Jerusalem, Otto insisted that we had to see the only Egyptian Coptic site in the city. We groaned, but his enthusiasm was infectious. We arranged to see the site the next morning.

Contrary to our expectations, it turned out to be a truly lovely moment. Otto knew of this single Coptic shrine outside the city walls, which marked some place where Jesus was supposed to have done something; I don't recall just what. A round, gold-colored metal ring in the earth designated the exact spot where whatever Jesus did was now venerated. One aged attendant who lived in a nearby wooden hut throughout the year greeted visitors and sold votive candles. Because the spot was outside the city walls and not near anything else of interest, visitors were rare.

The Egyptian jumped up as we approached, recognized Otto, and gave him a big hug, then went into a little speech in Coptic that he had memorized but seldom gave. Otto summarized it for us, and we all tried to look appreciative of the honor of visiting this spot. Finally, we asked if we could buy candles to light and carry our prayers to God. The attendant rushed into his shack to bring several boxes. We lit our candles, made solemn faces, and dug into our pockets to pay what was probably three or four times the price of the candles. The Egyptian beamed and blessed us each individually.

So it hadn't been such a bad day after all.

Otto did not take our group to the Gordon's Garden Tomb, which he considered a commercialization of faith. But when I was in Jerusalem on a later visit, I decided to pay a visit. "Pay" is an accurate word: there was an expensive ticket plus a gift shop to negotiate. Visitors walked through a manicured olive orchard with tiny speakers demurely sounding the recorded songs of local birds. The path led to a genuine rock-cut Jewish tomb, of which many still survive, with a stone rolled out of the way and a wooden burial platform inside. Americans who have grown up with nineteenth and early twentieth century pictures in their Sunday schools and churches were much more comfortable visiting the Garden Tomb than fighting the crowds and dirty monks in the Church of the Sepulcher.

So the lesson? When "reality" differs from illusion, we always have the option of changing an uncomfortable reality.

CYPRUS, PART 1
Before the Coup

CHAPTER 6

A Quiet Time of Meditation and Prayer

In 1971, my first wife and I were assigned from Athens to Nicosia. We'd just had our first child, but our marriage was shaky. We carried the tension with us to Cyprus, hoping somehow it would resolve itself, but, of course, it did not, and within a couple of months of our arrival, my wife packed up her and our daughter's things, bought tickets, and planned their return to the States.

Knowing the aftermath of their departure would be difficult, I spoke to the senior man on my staff and asked him, without explaining why, whether I could go to the island's largest and coincidentally wealthiest monastery for a few days of quiet relaxation. He made the arrangements and suggested that I take a gift for the abbot as a token of my appreciation. When I asked him what I should take, he said with a conspiratorial smile, "A few bottles of good Scotch whiskey." I silently wondered just how understanding of my intentions the good abbot might be. Nevertheless, I bought the whiskey at our local diplomatic stores and put it in the trunk.

A few days later, I went through the trauma of leave-taking at the airport. After seeing my wife and daughter onto the plane,

I left the airport and, at the intersection with the highway to the city, turned left onto the road leading up to the Troodos Mountains and Kykos Monastery.

I arrived at Kykos in midafternoon. As an expected guest of some diplomatic importance, I was met in the parking lot by the monastery guest master. I'd visited numerous monasteries in Greece and was never particularly impressed with the neatness or cleanliness of the monks. So I was somewhat surprised by this monk.

Brother Sotiris wore a clean white shirt under his black monk's robe; the starched white collar was visible above the robe. Also, formal French style cuffs complete with cufflinks were visible at the ends of the robe's sleeves. If I had thought that monks were really into poverty, chastity, and charity (I already knew better), this confirmed that Sotiris was of a different cut than your average small Greek monastery monk. I was also interested that his name was "Sotiris," which translated means "saved" (in the context of salvation.) I had no idea how interesting that appellation would be....

I opened the trunk to get my small bag and the gift for the abbot. Brother Sotiris grinned broadly and waved to an acolyte to come pick up the gift box, and I saw the boy trudge away with his load, presumably to the abbot.

Picking up my bag, I followed Sotiris to a spacious second-story room overlooking the forested hills. I expressed some mild surprise at the luxurious quarters: a native pine-paneled room with a large bed, my own small woodstove with an accompanying box of kindling and small logs, a private bath, thick plush bath towels, and a comfortable chair. Putting my things down, I explained to the monk that I had been under some stress lately and had come to relax and pray. He nodded but observed, "Well, that's understandable, Mr. Grimland, but we were told you would take your meals in the rectory with the abbot and my brother monks. Surely you don't have to pray *and* fast?"

"Oh no, Brother," I responded. "I would be honored to share a small meal with you all. Is it proper that I pay my respects to the abbot before dinner?"

"We do not follow a diplomatic protocol here," Sotiris said. "You are expected, and the Holy Father will meet you at dinner. That will be at seven o'clock, and I'll send the boy to show you the way. Until then, you may visit the chapel if you wish. You saw it as we came to your room?" I nodded, and the monk smiled and closed the door. I decided to lie down for half an hour's rest and then went down to the chapel, where I sat in silence for another half hour before returning to my room to get ready for dinner.

Promptly at seven, the boy appeared and shyly led me down to the dining hall. As I walked in, I could see the other monks, perhaps fifteen altogether, seated at the table, but before there was any chance for introductions, they all stood and faced the door, having seen the abbot arriving. I was introduced; one didn't use his name but called him "Pater." He greeted me and asked me to follow him to the seat on his right.

Throughout this visit I inserted Greek words or sentences, since I'd been used to using them when I was in Greece. And since I'd visited many monasteries, I'd seen the small smiles indicating a pleased reaction from the monks. I thought it made a better impression, since it showed that I'd made the effort to learn their language instead of expecting all of them to know English.

The refectory was large but not overwhelming. A long marble table set with china and crystal occupied the middle of the room. Ornately carved wooden chairs circled the table, and an acolyte pulled out the one at the head of the table for the abbot, who took his seat of honor. Another boy pulled out my chair, and when I was seated, the others took their places.

Several boys brought around brass bowls of warm water and hand towels, enough for every three monks, and we all washed and dried our hands. The abbot began a longish blessing with formulaic responses from the others, and when he'd finished, the boys began serving a hot soup. I hadn't been to many five-star hotels yet in my career, but the ones I had eaten in didn't hold a candle to the service at this "humble" monastery.

The rest of the meal followed: large baskets of bread, a vegetable course (some kind of greens), and an odd presentation of medium-sized fresh onions, with the roots and dirt still on the bulbs. I assumed this was to demonstrate their freshness, but they were served "naked" on our salad plates, and I watched the others, who used a fork and a sharp knife to cut the roots off the bulbs, wipe the dirt (or most of it) off the onion with their napkin, and finally put the cleaned (?) onion on a separate plate to slice and eat it. Some of the monks merely picked up and bit into the onions like apples. The abbot, of course, had an acolyte wash the freshly cleaned onion in one of the bowls of water for him and me. Then he used his knife and fork to slice the onion rather than picking it up apple-style. I followed suit.

A large bowl of well-flavored meat stew followed, ladled over a mound of rice. All this time the abbot was making polite conversation with me. I remember little of the conversation, but I made appropriate replies. He seemed to be most interested in how I had learned Greek, since it was obvious from my name that I was not a Greek American. I explained how our foreign service intensive language instruction was done and then added that I had spent three years in Greece learning to really use the language.

I noted, however, that I had been surprised that Greek Cypriots spoke with a distinctly different dialect than mainland Greeks and that I sometimes had difficulty understanding them. He proudly admitted that was so. "Our Greek is richer," he said. "We have absorbed more words and expressions from our Arab neighbors and our large Armenian population. We even have quite a few classical Greek words in our common vocabulary." I found it interesting that he didn't mention any influence from the twenty percent of Cyprus' population that was of Turkish origin from the days when the Ottoman Empire ruled the whole eastern Mediterranean littoral, but decided not to go there. I had absorbed the maxim that in talking with others, it is best to avoid the subjects of politics, religion, and sex.

Attempting to compliment the abbot, I admitted being a little surprised at the luxurious room I was given and the rather sophisticated attire of Brother Sotiris. "Ah, yes," replied the abbot, "our monks are quite well educated and have duties required of them which call on that education. We have a man who's an expert in machinery, another who's an agricultural specialist, a forestry expert, and a couple of accountants to maintain the books. We watch our expenses and income rather carefully. We own a good deal of land leased to peasants and must be watchful that we are not cheated by careless tenants."

"We are used to dealing with rather large sums of money and investments," he said. "As a matter of fact, with careful management we were able to purchase a submarine for our beloved Greece's navy last year."

I didn't know quite how to respond. I silently wondered what the purchase of a submarine had to do with Jesus' religion of peace, but to have raised the issue would have gotten us into politics *and* religion. Arms, wars, and conquest had always been a part of Christendom and certainly weren't limited to the Greeks, but I was astonished at what it must have cost to buy a submarine, even a used one, to donate to their brothers in Greece.

As we talked and ate, I noticed the abbot trying to unobtrusively glance at his watch. As soon as he politely could, he said to me, "Well, Mr. Grimland, we usually have our after-dinner coffee at the little *cafenio* you probably saw across from the entrance to the monastery. Would you care to accompany us?"

I did, of course, and we all trooped out and across the parking lot to the *cafenio*. A few other village customers, mostly laborers by the looks of their clothes, were already there, but tables had been saved for the monks. Most were watching the clock and glancing at the black and white television mounted high on the wall. The last program they'd been watching was just finishing. Ordering their coffee, the monks arranged themselves in what was obviously an oft-repeated pattern, the most central chairs reserved for the abbot and me.

I asked the abbot what we were expecting on the TV. "Oh, they run an American comedy series every week," he said. "It's called *Archie Bunker and His Family*. You must have seen it. We think it is indeed hilarious."

I admitted that I had indeed seen *All in the Family* and enjoyed it. "But," I asked, 'is the program in English?" Many Cypriots spoke English, and imported programs on Cyprus television frequently were broadcast without going to the expense of subtitling them into Greek. The abbot replied, "No, there are subtitles. Many of the funny parts are in your New York dialect and are hard to follow for those who have not lived in that city."

The music on the TV clued our little audience that *Archie Bunker* was about to start; the monks were already chuckling in anticipation of Archie, Edith, and Meathead's New York humor. Just as the titles came on, one of the other customers, a villager, shifted his chair for a better view and accidentally kicked the cord that plugged the television into the wall. Moans of disappointment from everyone, shouts of "What happened?" and "For the love of God, fix it!" filled the room until the poor guy who'd nearly caused the disaster figured out what he'd done and plugged the set back in—sighs of relief all around.

I noticed that some of the monks had ordered the strong, anise-flavored *ouzo* after their coffee and were already giggling at anything that moved on the television screen. The momentary loss of power had particularly distressed them. But in the presence of the abbot, they kept their comments to themselves—I thought mainly not to give away to me that they'd been imbibing. I could have cared less whether they were drinking, but perhaps my exalted status as a guest expecting spiritual comfort inhibited them from murdering the offending customer who might have deprived them of *Archie Bunker.* Undoubtedly the miscreant had no idea that my presence may have saved his life.

I'd never watched television with Greek monks, and certainly not a subtitled version of Archie Bunker. I could understand the English, of course, but found it hard to follow most of the subtitles since the lines were fast-paced, and the subtitles considerably shorter than the dialogue. But I caught enough to recognize some rather odd translations. In many places, the subtitles bore no relationship to the actors' spoken lines. But what was interesting was that the monks and abbot guffawed for almost the entire half hour of Archie's antics.

The show finished, and the monks picked up their robes and trudged back to the monastery. I asked whether there would be a service in the church that evening. It was still only about nine, but the abbot said, "On *Archie* nights, we allow ourselves a brief respite from our spiritual requirements. I trust you understand.

I did, of course, and was glad I wouldn't have to face a droning hour of chanting and censing in a chilly stone church. I bid my fellow revelers good night and returned to my room, where I found that someone had already started a fire in the stove and gotten the space comfortably warm. A bottle of the scotch I'd brought was set on the night table, with a clean glass, but since I had not acquired a taste for scotch yet (and never would), I decided not to partake of any "spiritual" comfort. My bed had been turned down. I was tired from the airport scene, the drive to Kykos, and being "on" all evening. My head hit the pillow, and I conked out for the night, realizing before I drifted off that I'd forgotten to ask about church the next morning.

I awoke later than usual and, after getting up and washing my face, heard a soft knock at the door. The acolyte (evidently I'd been assigned my own personal caretaker) was at the door with a basket of sesame-covered toasted rolls, some feta cheese, and sliced tomatoes, and a large glass of fresh-squeezed orange juice.

Taking the food, I asked when church began. "Brother Sotiris will be here a little later," the boy replied, "and explain the program for the day."

Program for the day? My intention had been to keep to myself except for one or two of the church services.

Well, Sotiris indeed showed up and said that a number of his fellow monks had suggested we go quail hunting. I explained that I had neither a gun nor a hunting license. He assured me that they had an extra shotgun and shells, and that a license was not necessary (that comment was delivered with a wink) on monastery property. I had hoped to spend the day walking in the wooded hills and coming to terms with my new loss but realized that my priority in this situation had to be one of being a good guest. So I agreed, and, almost immediately, five other monks materialized from wherever they'd been waiting, presented me with my gun and a shooting bag, and off we went.

I'd hunted quail as a kid in Texas and knew how to flush the birds out and shoot, but, oddly, the monks seemed like a group of boys on a lark with stick guns. They walked in no particular order, one or two often obscured by the trees and undergrowth from seeing the others. When any one of them flushed a bird, it sounded like the Normandy invasion as four or five double-barreled shotguns blasted off in quick succession. I was a little far away but could see no birds fall. Apparently my fellow hunters were out for the bang, not the bird.

After several volleys, there probably wasn't a quail within twenty miles of us, but Sotiris shouted that his comrades had to return and give the guest a chance. So after impressing on them that I preferred they walk where I could see them and that they *not* shoot, we set off on the hilly ground again. I didn't expect to see so much as a feather of a bird, but evidently the quail were so confused by all the shots coming from so many directions, that they'd simply hunkered down and tried to blend into the scrub brush and grass. I hadn't walked more than fifty yards when a lone bird, wildly flapping its wings, rose up almost vertically. As I aimed, leading the bird in flight, I heard Sotiris shouting to the others to be careful and hold their fire. I was glad we'd had no time to develop any grudges....

I pulled the trigger, and down the bird went. Applause from my companions echoed off the hills, while an acolyte "bird dog" ran to pick up the dead bird and deposit it into my hunting bag.

Again we set out, again the same sequence of scenes and another bird dumped in my bag. The good thing for me about quail hunting was that the birds are shot at close range, so it's easy to be accurate and get a clean kill.

The monks seemed to be having a great time even though they weren't shooting. Indeed, I occasionally glanced back and saw them uncork small hip flasks to lubricate the mood. With about a dozen birds in my bag I decided it would be foolish to press my luck and take the chance that a somewhat inebriated monk would be unable to not shoot. I announced that I'd had enough and was hungry for lunch.

Back we all trooped, the others oddly heady for my success but in fact already salivating at the thought of quail for our little band of brothers' dinner that night. No communal onions and stew—we had some real man kill meat, man eat meat.

It was way beyond lunchtime by the time we hiked back to the monastery. I began to get a low-sugar headache and surreptitiously grabbed bites of the single energy bar I'd stuck in my pocket. Sotiris gave the boy orders to bring me some bread, cheese, and tomatoes to tide me through until dinner, and then he announced that everyone was invited back to my room at eight for the feast. They took the birds and disappeared, merrily chattering about what an interesting way it was to hunt: "Such organization! Such fine shooting on the part of our guest! He must really be a Texan—only Texans can shoot that well!"

They were exhilarated by the morning's exertions, but I was exhausted. They really weren't a bad lot: after all; they could organize themselves and marshal funds to purchase a submarine. Who was I to judge?

That evening, a sous-chef arrived at my room with the makings of dinner. Noticing that the bottle of scotch had remained unopened, he asked whether I'd like a beer with dinner or some monastery wine, some *ouzo* or—and he grinned—a special surprise. Still determined to be a good guest, I agreed to the special surprise. He left as the group of hunters arrived, Sotiris in the lead, each bearing his own bottle or flask of pre-dinner libation and an offering of nuts or cheese and bread to whet our appetites. We chatted—they had not heard my conversation with the abbot on the previous evening and proudly spoke of their respective special duties.

A little foolishly, I asked how they purified their drinking water, "Ah, God cleans the water: it comes from two holy springs below the monastery that were part of the land granted by the Byzantine emperor himself. It is said that he drank of the water and was given new virility to produce more sons!" (Nudge, nudge ...) "By the way, we hear that you have chosen to try our special surprise to drink? Here it is!" Sotiris produced a clear bottle of liquid; glasses for all appeared from somewhere, and a full glass (not a shot) of clear liquid was poured. Knowing that *ouzo* was sometimes drunk without ice, I didn't ask, but after several handfuls of nuts, all raised their glasses and toasted me, Texas, Archie Bunker, the abbot, baby Jesus—the list went on as everyone worked up to the finale. Finally, they started downing the hatch, and I—a little more cautious—took a sip of my drink.

God! The stuff was strong enough to knock out a mule. I choked and managed to gasp, "What *is* that?"

"*Zivania!*" they chorused. "The finest in Cyprus. And available only here at Kykos for special occasions."

My eyes tearing, I managed another few sips before reaching for a glass of water to dilute the stuff.

At this moment the boys arrived with the quail dinner. I hoped it would distract my company for the rest of the evening. The waiter had the quail arranged on a large platter. They'd been plucked and cleaned but with a couple of curious omissions. They lay on their backs with their tiny feet and claws sticking up in the air. The cook had arranged the birds in a circle with the plucked, naked heads draped artistically over the edges of the platter. As he set the platter down in the middle of our group, I was eyeball to eyeball with a couple of the birds staring accusingly at me. My companions picked them up by the little feet and began to eat them whole: bones, feet, heads, beaks— everything. The only sound was the loud smacking of lips and the muffled appreciation of the diners. I admit that the birds tasted delicious once I got past the eyeballs and managed to discretely spit the heads and feet into my napkin.

But the *zivania* devil had not yet been exorcised. Sotiris piped up:

"Mr. David, you should try the *zivania* in the traditional Cypriot way!"

"Oh, great, brother. Does that make it stronger?"

"Of course not; it just adds flavor. Watch!"

With that, one of the monks held out his palm, another pulled a black pepper grinder out of his robe pocket, and a third produced a flask of something clear that smelled suspiciously like vinegar. Sotiris merely watched, a mischievous smile on his face.

"Christ himself was offered vinegar on the cross," one said. "We can do no less!"

He took the glass of *zivania*, poured about half of it back into the bottle, and chugalugged it. No sooner had he swallowed it than he licked the crushed black pepper off his palm and, taking the half-glass of vinegar, drank it straight as a chaser.

"I can't do this," I thought. "I'll throw it up."

But I'd crossed the Rubicon: there was no turning back on the Special Surprise drunk in the traditional way. Sotiris took charge. He poured me a large glass of *zivania*—and I promptly poured back all but the smallest amount I could hold in the glass. Someone ground a little black pepper into my palm, and the vinegar chaser was readied. I'd come for meditation and prayer, so I prayed: "God, *please* let this cup pass from me!" ... swallowing the *zivania*, I licked the pepper off my hand and tossed back the small amount of vinegar in the glass. I was right: it was ghastly. But I held it down while the little room, heated to sweat-lodge temperatures by human bodies and the little woodstove, spun around my field of vision. But I still held it down; I'd passed whatever test had been required to prove my manhood—my defense of the Alamo, my worthiness to be knighted into the Circle of Sweat. Thank God I didn't have to do it again!

Sotiris grinned and said, "Ah, Brother Dave: now you too have been truly saved. Live well, my friend!"

I suppose I should have felt honored, but I was still talking my stomach into cooperating and not rejecting my "salvation."

I'd planned when I left Nicosia to spend three or four days at the monastery, but I hadn't told anyone else of my time frame. After attending church the next morning and undergoing the requisite censing and blessing, I decided my stress was much better, so I told the abbot that I'd better be getting back to work in Nicosia. He smiled and assured me that I'd be welcome back at any time, even adding that no "house gift" was necessary. Just be sure to come on a night when Archie and company were on the television.

While I was aware that I'd hardly gotten the peace and quiet I'd come for, perhaps I'd come away with something else. I'd gotten so distracted by the diversions that my emotional pain was no longer as intense as it was when I arrived.

Yes, the Lord works in mysterious ways—and takes care of his dumb animals in spite of ourselves.

CHAPTER 7

The Paris of the Middle East

Sometimes, somewhere, one does something just right. For whatever reason that something—often a small gesture—resonates. Its quality, like good wine, improves with age. But sometimes that undeniably beautiful moment exists simultaneously with an underlying darkness of a society in decay.

Beirut, 1971. The St. George Hotel.

I'd flown in that day from Cyprus on my way to a conference in Pakistan. We arrived a little before lunch to what was then no doubt the Levant's most cosmopolitan city: often called, by those who live in the Middle East and Europeans alike, "The Paris of the Middle East." I'd booked a reservation at the St. George, a faded but still gracious old French-style hotel in the heart of a city that, sadly, in just a few years, would descend into political tribalism, anarchy, and gruesome sectarian murder. As an outsider, I did not recognize in my first glimpse of this old hotel the disturbing signs of *fin de siècle*: the end of old French civility. Like Germany in the late 1930s, Lebanon was increasingly tainted with decadence. I was to witness the sexual decadence later that evening, but the political shift would not be apparent to outsiders for another six years.

As soon as I checked in at the St. George, I went walking and stopped in a local cheap eatery to try sheep's testicles. Ever since I was a child in Texas, I'd known that the best food was often served in the least pretentious cafes, where the local menu items were frequently offered with the owner's or cook's special condiments or spices.

Returning in midafternoon to my elegantly faded room, I noticed a pamphlet that offered tours of Beirut. So I called the reception desk and signed up for an evening bus tour that included the internationally famous *Casino du Liban*. The tour included dinner and a ticket to the cabaret. This Parisian-style floor show had been produced by the *Folies Bergere* in Paris, and the casino was as well-known for its extravagant shows as it was for its gambling.

Since the bus wouldn't pick me up until eight for the hour's ride to the casino and cabaret, I knew I'd get hungry before. So at the unreasonably early hour of 6:30 p.m., I went down to the St. George's restaurant for a snack.

At that hour, I was the only customer. With starched linen tablecloths, silver-plate utensils, a faux leather-covered menu, and three waiters hovering over me, I sensed there was no way I could just have a snack. So I ordered a fresh lobster with melted butter and lemon on the side. In a flourish of pseudo-sophistication—I was all of twenty-five years old and looked it—I also ordered a bottle of Saint Emilion, a French red wine I had enjoyed on special occasions with American friends in Greece. "Hell," I thought, "I know I'm supposed to have white wine or champagne with the lobster, but I'm more in the mood for red."

The St. Emilion was a class touch that I felt would pass the sophistication test of the otherwise unoccupied waiters and uphold the honor of American civilization. I hadn't counted on the pianist as a player in this test of my sophistication.

No sooner had I ordered than he quietly appeared—obviously waiting for the first customer of the evening. He was formally dressed, tuxedo and black tie, and he sat down at the seven-foot Steinway grand with a quiet graciousness that gave no hint that I was his only listener. I had no idea whether he was French, but he carried himself with quiet dignity. And then he began to play.

First some light Broadway tunes. He glanced at me. I smiled appreciatively, and he switched to Chopin. Then to Mozart.

I don't know why, but almost without thinking I asked the waiter to pour the pianist a glass of the excellent St. Emilion I'd been drinking. The waiter disappeared, and returned with a small silver tray and a sparkling crystal red wine glass. Carefully arranging the starched linen napkin around the wine bottle, he poured the artist a glass, taking it quietly across the room and leaving it on top of the Steinway.

The pianist finished the piece, looked at me, smiling gently—and taking the glass with graceful care and attention raised it slowly in *santé* to me. I raised my glass back, and we both drank to whatever had passed between us. Sometimes, somehow, one captures the moment just right.

The pianist and I finished about half the wine and—again, in a gesture of pseudo-sophistication—I left a large-value Lebanese pound note on the table. Smiling at the waiters, I walked out with a single glass of wine to await my bus at the hotel lobby door. The waiters had been obviously pleased—impressed, I thought, with my generosity and *savoir faire*. At least I chose to interpret their smiles that way.

The ride out to the casino was uneventful. The dark houses lit only by television sets and streetlights became mildly exotic in the glow, enhanced by the lingering taste of the lobster and the warmth of the excellent wine. Arriving at the huge hotel and entertainment hall, I found my way to an empty seat at one of the tables, greeting the other guests, first in my flawless (or so I thought) Greek and then in English. I felt I could do no wrong....

Dinner was served. The lobster and *St. Emilion* overwhelmed whatever the indifferent menu was; after all, people had come for the show not the food. The lights dimmed, cueing the live orchestra to launch the first act.

The music was well-played; with a grandiose fanfare, the show began. On the huge stage, a group of bare-chested young men in tight vests and pants appeared. The music changed, and from the wings appeared an equal number of beautiful young women wearing tight, short skirts, high heels—and nothing else.

I must admit, bare-breasted women turn me on. While I was too far from the stage to make out the details, my imagination provided them as the girls began to dance seductively with the men. Sitting at the darkened table with the other tourists, I tried to look cool and suave, as though I saw this sort of thing every day.

The understated dance ended, and the bare-chested men and bare-breasted women disappeared, having accomplished their job of whetting the appetite of the audience.

The orchestra signaled a change of scenery and mood, and green spotlights highlighted a long semicircular covered runway extending from the stage into the audience. The house lights dimmed, the spotlights brightened, and the music turned to a jungle rhythm. As we watched, the runway cover disappeared, revealing water inside the "banks" of the runway. From the ceiling, perhaps forty feet above the runway, artificial trees loaded with live monkeys descended to the "jungle river" below, where black-suited stage hands unobtrusively appeared to release the hooks and cables that had lowered the plastic trees. As the house lights reappeared, the "jungle" took on an astonishing reality. I had switched sometime earlier to the not-so-bad dinner wine, and the effects of the wine filled in any gaps in the "reality" of this jungle river.

From either side of the stage, large doors slid silently open, and jungle riverboats emerged, each one carrying a beautiful cargo of (yes, more) bare-breasted girls artfully arranged around baskets of real fruit. The girls picked up the fruit, slowly and tantalizingly taking a seductive bite or two before giving the rest to the delighted monkeys who had come down in the plastic trees. The boat with its cargo of girls and fruit actually belched smoke, like an image from the *African Queen*. But Katherine Hepburn, except in the privacy of a bedroom, could never have looked like these girls.

As soon as the boats completed their circuit of the jungle river and disappeared, the "river" disappeared and bright spotlights lit up the stage. Pounding music signaled the entrance of thundering horses galloping across the stage. Riding the horses were young men who rode as though they had just raided an off-stage village and were carrying away, I wanted to believe, willing girls.

No sooner had these village virgins been stolen away than the scene changed again. A huge fish tank rose slowly up from below the stage. In the tank were two live dolphins cavorting with four seemingly nude maidens, each with different colored long hair streaming down and offering tantalizing glimpses of more bare breasts. It took a few minutes of close attention to realize that each maiden was wearing skintight but modestly clouded plastic bikini bottoms that barely covered the area where legs met torso. Frankly, no one was looking at the dolphins.

I felt a momentary sadness for the fish. I know: dolphins aren't "fish," but with the distractions competing for my attention, I didn't debate the biology. I'm sitting there watching an excitingly sexual scene and feeling sorry for the fish? I sensed a fleeting feeling of discomfort but had no chance to examine why.

After only fifteen minutes or so of the cavorting dolphins and the maidens, the tank slowly sank back into the stage's basement, and the music signaled the finale was beginning. Spotlights drew the audience's attention up to the forty-foot-high ceiling. From what had appeared at first to be merely decorative patterns, some twenty or so circular discs began a slow descent, each bearing its own bare-breasted maiden slithering around the three-foot-diameter disc, each seminude girl wrapping herself around one of the supporting cables in a demure version of a pole dancer. The audience applauded wildly as the discs touched the floor of the hall. The girls leapt off whenever a disc touched the floor and moved slowly through the audience, carefully but gracefully avoiding the salivating men now on their feet and applauding. Unfortunately—or perhaps fortunately—none came within my reach. Frankly, I wouldn't have known what to do with one of these heavenly beauties had I caught one.

With the disappearance of the girls and a finale of rousing music from the orchestra, the show was obviously over. All that effort and expense had lasted for only about an hour. I admit it was sexy: no red-blooded twenty-five-year-old could have reacted differently. But there was also an uncomfortable feeling of excess: woven in with the sexuality was more than an undertone of decadence. I could not escape the feeling that I was watching a porn movie, that somehow I had been manipulated: the wine, the lighting, the music—all were deliberately combined to slowly increase my willingness to suspend disbelief. But the show had been sexy and fast-paced, and I hadn't time to examine the vague discomfort of which, writing this forty-five years later, I now am more aware.

Now the waiters began politely shepherding the still-excited tourists down to the basement, where the reason for the relatively brief show became apparent. The real money-maker, the gambling casino, was already in quiet but serious operation.

Just inside the fake art deco entrance, we passed three cashiers behind barred windows for those wishing to change Lebanese *pounds*, Japanese *yen*, Saudi *rials*, Greek *drachmas*—any amount of any national cash—into chips of different colors. On the right was a string of a dozen slot machines with cheap metal tokens available for those who wished to play for small sums. In the darkness beyond, green-covered tables sat, each in its own pool of light from a single covered lamp hanging over each table. I passed on the slots, figuring I didn't know how to gamble well enough to keep from losing my small cache of US dollars. I was more interested in getting to the tables and gawking. Waiters with trays of free drinks quietly saw to it that everyone's thirst was satisfied. Alcohol clouds rational thinking about the odds. Perhaps this was why most *sheiks* were drinking fruit juice: the Muslim prohibition against alcohol kept their heads clearer.

Most of the gamblers seated around the tables, the Arab *sheiks*, were dressed in expensive white robes, *kefiyas* of different colors and patterns that denoted nationality, and dark glasses. Behind each *sheik* was a clutch of dark-glassed security men, each visually checking the gawkers and also scanning the room for anyone suspicious.

On each table was a pile—I was astonished—of plastic chips: gold chips signifying $1,000, silver worth $500, blue $100, and "pocket change" red chips at $50. Most of the piles were exclusively gold and silver chips, and the game appeared to be straight blackjack. There was no talking; the *sheiks* conveyed their desire for a card or a pass by a slight raising of one or two fingers when the green-visored dealer indicated it was their turn. This was serious business, although I supposed it was considered fun by these wealthy players.

After a half hour of watching the games at different tables but thinking of those lovely dolphins, I decided "What the hell. I can't come to the Paris of the Middle East and be too cheap to try my luck with $50!" So I returned to the cashiers and exchanged a $50 bill for five metal slot machine tokens.

Having never played the one-armed bandits before, I had no idea what combination of symbols signified a win or a loss. I only remembered reading somewhere that three lemons was a loser. But I was determined to lose $50, so I slipped a $10 token into one of the machines and pulled the lever. The spinning gears inside clicked off the appointed seconds and stopped. Nothing clinked into the payoff drawer at the bottom. A few fellow neophytes gathered behind me hoping to figure out how to play the odds.

I tried again, inserting another $10 coin into the machine and pulling the lever. This time three metal tokens fell into the payoff bin. I quickly (and mistakenly) calculated I was $20 ahead! I felt the rush to feed the machine again: *I was on a roll!* I went to another machine, determined to walk away with a thousand dollars' worth of tokens. I could see myself returning to the St. George and tipping everyone lavishly, with enough left over to buy a new car I didn't even need when I returned to Cyprus.

Again, I felt that fleeting sense of being manipulated by the free alcohol and the darkness and gaudy décor, created with painted plaster instead of marble and wood; my spendthrift demon was having his chain jerked. My sensible angel appeared and cast out my short-term wealth demon. I turned around and went back to the cashier, who rather disdainfully accepted my remaining tokens. He must have seen too many bitten by the lure of easy riches—the seductive power to spend easy gains on unnecessary ego enhancement. The cashier seldom got one like me who came to his senses early.

CYPRUS, PART 2

The Coup, Riots, and an Assassination

CHAPTER 8

How Quickly a Coup Can Change Life

What was originally an interesting assignment on Cyprus, a sleepy Mediterranean island, suddenly turned into a year's nightmare.

The island nation was divided unevenly between the Greek Cypriots and the Turkish Cypriots under a deal brokered by the British in 1960, who took as their brokerage fee operational rights to a large airbase on the island's southeast corner facing Syria, Lebanon, and Israel. The base was exceptionally useful as an intelligence-gathering operation for events in the Middle East, both by telephonic interception and later by American U-2 spy aircraft. So the British and Americans, not to mention the Greek and Turkish Cypriots and their mainland "mother" countries, all had a stake in the island.

In 1974, the Greek Cypriot ultranationalists, with the help of the mainland right-wing Greek junta in Athens, decided it was time to instigate a coup to get rid of Archbishop and President Makarios. Makarios had a reputation of playing his cards craftily: he had to balance the competing interests of Greek and Turkish Cypriots and their respective mainland "protectors," the British, Americans, and—would you believe—the Chinese and Soviets. He had only a small national guard to depend on; its officers were mainland Greeks. But he had remained an adept negotiator and was reputed to be a wealthy man by taking fees and taxes from all but being parsimonious about distributing the largess.

The Greeks and Greek Cypriots considered him a slippery character, an obstacle to their not so underlying goal of *enosis* or union of the island with Greece. Already surrounded by Greek islands, mainland Turkey was strongly opposed to any such plan.

Immediately following an unsuccessful effort to kill the archbishop, the shooting seemed to lessen, and I called the embassy on my two-way radio, receiving the ambassador's permission to get our local employees out of our official cultural center. I decided to evacuate my American secretary and two of our Turkish Cypriot staffers who didn't have a safe way back to their side of the divided city. The others felt they could make it home on their own.

My worried American secretary had left her four-year-old daughter with a housekeeper at her home near the presidential palace, scene of Makarios' compound and likely some of the heaviest fighting. As we drove slowly past groups of frightened Greek Cypriot civilians, we encountered a checkpoint manned by a nervous young Greek Cypriot National Guardsman. Stopping well short of the armed soldier, I got out of the car with my hands up, and, speaking Greek more calmly than I felt, explained that we had to get past his checkpoint to check my secretary's house for the child. He listened to my story and then leveled his automatic rifle at me.

"My officer has told me that no one is allowed past my checkpoint," he insisted. Nothing I could immediately think of trumped this argument ... so I waited a few seconds, and it finally came to me: Greeks loved children.

"I understand your officer's order," I said, "but I'm sure he would allow me to take a mother to her frightened baby." I repeated this, stressing the word *moro* ("baby"), and I could see the young soldier wavering, torn between his orders and his deeper cultural training.

Finally I offered, "Look: I'll leave the mother here in the car and walk to her house. It's right there, less than a hundred meters away. I'll bring the baby and nanny back here, and then we'll leave. You can watch me the whole time."

He thought about it for what seemed like an eternity and finally jerked his head in assent.

"Go. But I'm watching you—and I have a gun...."

Emphasizing his point, he pulled the bolt back to cocked position.

Mentally thanking my Greek teachers, I said, "I understand. God bless you for your kindness."

Walking with my hands in the air, I wondered nervously how it felt to be shot in the back. The house was open but deserted. It appeared that at the first sign of trouble, the frightened housekeeper had taken the child and run to her own house several blocks away. I returned to the car and guard, thanked him and drove a few blocks in a different direction, where we found the little girl at the housekeeper's home, happily eating bread and jam. With mother and daughter united, I took them to my home to stay with my wife, and reinforce their mutual confidence.

The Greek Cypriot nationalists, supported by the mainland Greek government, itself a junta that had come to power in a coup in Greece four years earlier, named as president of the Greek Cypriot population a man I'd known as a right-wing newspaper publisher who favored Greek Cypriot union with Greece. I can think of no kinder thing to say about Nikos Sampson than that he was an obnoxious thug. He had a reputation of being an enthusiastic killer of Turkish Cypriots. He was popular, however, with a significant group of ultranationalists and therefore had never been brought to justice by the Greek Cypriot police or courts.

So with Makarios gone and Nikos Samson as acting president until elections could be called, the mainland Turks, watching events across forty miles of the Mediterranean Sea, thought they could see the handwriting on the wall. Sampson did not last long.

Less than a week after the coup, mainland Turkish troops invaded the island, partially to protect the frightened minority Turkish Cypriot communities. However, the invasion served two purposes: by occupying the northern forty-five percent of the island, the Turks could count on the fifty thousand Greek Cypriots residing there to flee south, thus ensuring the safety of the Turkish Cypriots who stayed; and, in view of the fact that Turkish Cypriots were only twenty percent of the island's population, it gave the Greeks an excuse to cry "unfair," creating a political and public relations disaster that still lingers.

CHAPTER 9

Saving an Old Ship

My job up to this point had been to maintain contacts with the local Greek Cypriot journalists and cultural figures. The Turkish Cypriots had, several years before, barricaded themselves into small enclaves, mainly in the northern part of the island near Mother Turkey.

Most of our USIA work on the island was "public affairs" diplomacy, the term for harmless programming designed to "tell America's story to the world." We did not have an overtly political or economic or intelligence-gathering agenda—mainly a cultural program centered on an American library in downtown Nicosia, separate from the US Embassy.

All this changed with the July 14, 1974, coup and subsequent Turkish invasion.

When the invasion began, several American friends of mine were working in an old Venetian castle on the northern coast. A few years before, a Greek Cypriot sponge diver had found what turned out to be a fourth century BCE wooden coastal freighter on the sea floor in less than a hundred feet of water. The Americans had laid out a grid of pipes to photograph and map the wreck, thereby enabling them to methodically map the artifacts.

Underwater archaeology was still in its infancy; the archaeologists were careful about locating and raising the old ship's timbers, but they quickly learned that when exposed to air, water-soaked timbers and artifacts would soon disintegrate as the seawater in the cellular structure of the timbers dried out. So they began to immerse the timbers in a glycerol solution that replaced the seawater with the waxy glycerol that, when dry, solidified to the consistency of candle wax and prevented the wood from turning to dust. They had huge vats of this solution in the castle near the town of Kyrenia.

They began to reassemble the ship piece by piece, learning first that these ships had been built shell-first. The strakes were bent and curved and fitted together by the mortise and tendon method, and built up from the keel. Then the ancient shipbuilders would fit the ribs into the shell and cover the whole affair with a deck. Finally the cracks between the joints would be stuffed with oiled rags or small rope. This method of construction, unknown until then, made the ship flex more in stormy seas.

The wreck contained little of monetary value—they found only isolated coins and utilitarian cups, no major gold or silver—but the scientific and historical knowledge was priceless. Altogether they had raised and reassembled about three-quarters of the ship by the time of the invasion, identifying the crew's galley and some waterlogged provisions and what appeared to be low-fired clay amphorae of wine and oil. Most identifiable were the almonds. Except for being blackened by the glycerol solution, they looked as fresh in their shells as if they'd been harvested that day instead of three hundred to four hundred years before Jesus' disciples fished the Lake of Galilee, probably in boats made in the same way.

It was a simple vessel meant for hauling bulk freight of pottery, lumber, olive oil, and wine. Marks on the bow and sides appeared to show signs of a battle, perhaps with pirates:

arrow points that helped date the ship to the late Bronze Age, scratches made from grappling hooks, a mast partially chopped away—all pointed to a brief but deadly fight for possession of the ship's cargo.

The castle's thick walls protected the ship from melting most of the year. But in the hot Cypriot summers, the archaeologists had taken the precaution of installing air conditioners in the assembly room to guarantee that the temperature remained constant.

When the Turkish army invaded, they came ashore not far from the castle, and the first casualty was the loss of electrical power over most of northern Cyprus. So when I came back to my home in Nicosia one hot afternoon, I found that I had four refugee Americans sitting in my home. I knew them all from previous visits to their project and was glad they had chosen to stay with me. I needed the relief of company and someone with whom I could share food and wine.

I had enough spare beds and had managed to stock up on consumables from the few shops that braved the coup violence to stay open and feed people. Fortunately, even though the power was off, we did have emergency potable water, which I'd collected as soon as I could after the fighting started. Most of the food was fresh or canned, so the loss of power was not an immediate problem. The riots that would come in a few days at our embassy had not started yet—our ambassador would be assassinated in the first one—but between duty at the embassy, translating for the ambassador, and reporting to Washington, I had little time to play host.

My guests quickly came to the point. Without electricity to the auxiliary air conditioners in the castle, the partially reconstructed ship would soften and lose its shape; perhaps even come apart. Could I possibly do *anything*, they asked, to get the power turned on, just to the castle? They estimated that it would take about five days for the heat to build to the danger point. It seemed an unlikely possibility, but I promised to relay their concern to the ambassador and get back to them the next evening.

I went in the next morning and explained the problem to Ambassador Roger Davies. He called in our security staff and the defense attaché, and we stood around a wall map of the island. The road was no problem; it had not been shelled by the invading or defending forces. But we had to find the Turkish commander of the Kyrenia sector and talk him into working on the problem.

The ambassador finally spoke: "Dave, this is a worthwhile cultural issue in which we should give whatever help we can to the American researchers. I can loan you my limo, but the driver is Greek Cypriot, and he will be afraid to go into the Turkish-controlled sector. Even once you're in there, your language expertise is in Greek, not Turkish—you'll be on your own to find the right Turk to help. But if you're willing to try, we'll do all we can to back you up. I can't spare another American officer to go with you, but we'll stay in touch by radio. Are you willing to try?"

"Yes, sir. I will undoubtedly be safer in the Turkish-controlled sector, as there are no riots or other disturbances there, and I'm hopeful that I'll find enough Turkish officers to get me to the castle."

The defense attaché nodded. "Lots of Turkish officers have been on short-term NATO-sponsored training courses in the United States," he said, "and while the ordinary foot soldier may not know English, he'll respect the American flag on the ambassador's car, and help out."

Ambassador Davies added, "Why don't you talk to Mike Austrian (our only Turkish-speaking officer) and get a few words of Turkish under your belt—polite greetings, asking directions, that sort of stuff. You won't need to search for food; above all, Turks are hospitable."

I agreed and immediately sat down with Mike, pencil in hand, for my thirty-minute crash course in Turkish. It was daunting; Turkish was so utterly different from Greek or anything I'd ever heard. But at least the alphabet was in Western letters, and I was working on adrenalin now; the new linguistic forms seemed to stick.

I drove back to my house, reported the conversation to my guests, and began to throw a few clothes and some energy bars into a knapsack. One of the American archaeologists thought he should go with me, but I nixed that; he had no diplomatic passport, and the last thing I needed was to lose him to an overzealous guard.

Returning to the embassy, I traded in my Volkswagen van for the ambassador's armored Cadillac, a small American flag affixed to the front bumper. I felt as if I was driving a battleship. My colleagues waved me off—several probably wishing they could go for the glory. But there wouldn't be any glory if I failed.

I drove first to the Green Line checkpoint guarding the dividing line in the city between Greeks and Turks. The Greek guards had fled at the beginning of the coup; only the mainland Turks, crouched behind sandbag bunkers, were on duty. They stepped out as I drove up and asked me where I was going (I think). Slowly I managed to make them understand that I wanted to go to the Kyrenia *kale* (castle) and speak to the *bas comuntan* (senior commander).

Turkish isn't hard to pronounce, and the soldiers understood immediately. One of them mimed that he would get in the car for the forty-five-minute drive and take me directly to the commander in charge. Not seeing any problem with this, I waved him in, rifle and all. As we pulled away, he motioned to a tea shop that was open, but I had to shake my head. Time was precious. I turned on the air conditioner instead and offered him a warm Coke from my knapsack. He grinned; even warm Coke tasted good in an air-conditioned limo with flags flying.

My guide had no trouble getting us through the next couple of roadblocks—we looked too important for anyone to question. And sure enough, less than an hour later we pulled up to a commandeered hotel in the village of Kyrenia that served as the headquarters of the Turkish commander. My guide jumped out, ran around to open my car door and, taking me by the arm, guided me into the hotel.

The headquarters was controlled chaos. Message runners dashed in and out, radios crackled, and fighter jets roared above on their way to missions further south. None of it slowed my guide down. Five minutes later, I was waiting outside the office of the commandant.

A private offered us sweetened glasses of hot tea and packaged biscuits as we waited. Finally the door opened, and I was shown in. I decided to try my luck with English and, indeed, the colonel responded in flawless English. Taking a cue from my experience in Greece and Cyprus, I didn't plunge immediately into what was on my mind, nor did the colonel ask. Rather I complimented him on his English; he had trained at Fort Hood as part of a NATO exchange program. We asked about each other's marital status, health of children, and commented on the hot weather. Finally the colonel revealed his harried state of mind and asked how he could help.

I was only thirty years old and looked it. But I was the American ambassador's envoy and mustered up as much polite authority as I could. As succinctly as possible, I explained why I had come, finishing up with my request that he somehow get the power back on to the air conditioners in the castle.

He smiled. "Mr. Grimland, you're amazing. I'm in the middle of directing an invasion: I've got ships offshore ferrying in troops and supplies; I'm awaiting word from the field on any Greek resistance we're meeting, and you're sitting here asking me to get the air-conditioning in a *Greek* castle turned on to save a two-thousand-year-old *Greek* ship. It would be amusing if I had time to be amused."

"I see your point, sir, but you'll have to admit that it's a Venetian castle, and the ship may or may not have been Greek. It was a lowly freighter, owned possibly by Phoenicians or even Turks. It's a major advancement to science for us to save what is possibly Turkey's contribution to the history of shipbuilding."

Again he smiled, motioning the orderly to bring more tea and cookies. "Well, you make a compelling case, Mr. Grimland. Perhaps we should do what we can to help the world understand that Turkey may have played a role in the history of shipbuilding."

He picked up the radio beside him and barked some orders.

"My senior engineer will look into it. If there's been no damage to the equipment itself, we'll get it running in ten minutes. If it's been hit in the shelling, we can set up a large generator to supply enough power for just those two rooms. If it's cool in there, I may move my headquarters, and you can join us in comfort for the rest of the invasion!"

"You're very kind, Colonel, and I'd like nothing more than to accept your invitation, but I can't even make good Turkish tea, so I'll have to wait until I see you in Turkey someday to repay your kindness."

"*Inshallah!*" (God willing), he replied. "I know you're anxious to get back to your ambassador and report our excellent cooperation. I'll send an English-speaking escort with you so you'll have no delays."

He produced a small haversack with a fresh supply of cookies, some cold Coca-Cola, and a couple of tins of tuna fish. "*Hiyirli yolculuklar!*" (Good journey!), he said. "*Allah korusun.*" (May God protect you.) I understood nothing but caught the warmth of the good wishes. We shook hands, and I started to leave. "And by the way, the soldier who accompanied you from the checkpoint reported that your Turkish isn't bad for a Greek speaker. How long did you study it?"

"About thirty minutes, Colonel; I was in a bit of a rush to get here."

"Perhaps you'd like to stop by the castle and see for yourself that everything is all right?"

"No, thank you, Colonel. I'm sure if it's not, you'll make it so."

The return ride was even quicker than coming to Kyrenia. My guide and I got to know each other. He was a university student in Turkey, studying ancient Turkish history. We stopped for tea, and I offered to open one of the tins of tuna fish. "Oh, thank you, sir, but those are gifts from our commander. You must enjoy them in good health."

I pulled up at the checkpoint into the Greek sector, and we wished each other well. Driving immediately to the embassy, I reported "mission accomplished" to Ambassador Davies and offered him a package of Turkish cookies. He smiled and took it. I didn't know it, but it would be the last time I worked closely with him. The demonstrations at the embassy began about three weeks later, and, as described in chapter 10, Ambassador Davies and Toni Varvaras, a Greek Cypriot staffer, were both killed in the first riot.

But for now, flush with my success, I traded the limo back for my Volkswagen—Cinderella's gilded coach again become a pumpkin—and drove home to my guests, who, upon hearing my story, were deliriously happy. We celebrated that night with tuna fish and crackers and copious amounts of wine.

Six months or so later, after they'd returned to the castle, one of them showed up at my house one evening.

"Dave, in gratitude for your contribution to science and an improvement in our diet, we'd like you to have these two almonds from the ship. They're a little old for eating but something to remember what you did for us."

Today they still sit in a glass bottle in a special tray on our bookshelves, where I show them to visitors and ask them to tell me what they are. Many guess correctly, even though they are hardly the color of almonds. Depending on my sense of their interest and the time available, I'll either tell them the story or simply say, "Well once upon a time, I saved an old ship...."

CHAPTER 10

Our First Riot—and Our First Deaths

The Greek Cypriot population, having fled to the southern half of the island, now conveniently forgot that their side had upset the *status quo* with the coup, and instead blamed the United States for not stopping the Turkish invasion. Our embassy in Nicosia thus became a convenient target for Greek Cypriots to vent their frustration.

The first riot erupted on August 19, 1974—and proved deadly. Greek Cypriot ultranationalists used the noisy demonstration to divert attention from their gunshots in a successful assassination of our ambassador, Rodger Davies, and, by accident, a Greek Cypriot administrative assistant, Toni Varvaras.

I was not in the embassy when it was attacked, the ambassador having asked me to attend and report back after the first press conference given by newly named interim Greek Cypriot President Glafkos Clerides. During the press conference, my two-way radio beeped: our defense attaché was calling to tell me that Ambassador Davies had been shot, and rioters were still too numerous for an ambulance to get through. Could I drive to the Nicosia hospital and bring back a doctor?

I rushed from the room and hurriedly drove to the hospital in Nicosia. No luck; not a single doctor would get in the car with a now despised American, much less drive back to our embassy through hostile rioters. I radioed the embassy and learned that President Clerides had also left the press conference and driven to the embassy, where he volunteered to take Ambassador Davies to a nearby medical clinic used by many of the American staff because of the doctor's professional skill and welcoming manner.

At our defense attaché's request, I drove to the clinic. When I pulled up to the emergency entrance, Doctor Nikos came out and took me by the arm: "Stop hurrying, Dave. He's dead. He was dead when they got him here. Come, I'll take you to him."

I was stunned. Nikos had to take my arm and guide me to the examining room, leaving me there for a few moments to absorb the terrible truth.

Ambassador Davies lay on his back, a sheet covering the lower half of his body. Exactly over his heart was a single bullet hole, now wiped clean. His eyes had been closed—he looked peacefully asleep. I'd finally had enough; I broke down and wept.

Nikos returned and said, "They told me that Toni (the Greek Cypriot staffer) had been hit in the head by machine-gun fire and died instantly. The ambassador also died instantly. He was hit directly in the heart, but since the single rifle wound was small, no one realized that it was immediately fatal. The phones are down; I don't think anyone at the embassy knows yet."

I switched on my radio but heard only static. "I'd better get over there," I replied. "I can't raise anyone on the radio."

"God forgive us all," replied Nikos. "Please give his children my deepest condolences. There was nothing I could do."

"Of course, Nikos. Thank you for everything." I walked out, feeling the terrible weight of a vicious and unfair world.

Driving to the embassy's rear entrance I radioed the guard inside, giving him my security number, then walked the remaining twenty yards to the building. It seemed eerily quiet. A Marine in battle gear, carrying a loaded shotgun, opened a locked steel gate. His eyes asked "the question."

"He's dead," I said quietly. "I saw him."

The young Marine's eyes filled with tears. "Damn! God damned bastards ..."

He waved me in and jerked his thumb up.

"They're all upstairs," he said, "cleaning Toni's brains off the walls."

I went up the stairs, moving over to let one of the American officers descend with two buckets of bloody water. I repeated my news—again, a curse. I finally found the defense attaché and told him. He turned around and headed for the secure Communications Center.

"I'd better let Washington know .... Damn!"

Ambassador Rodger Davies was perhaps the finest diplomat it has ever been my pleasure and honor to work with. He had arrived in Cyprus a couple of months earlier with his two children, Dana, twenty, and John, fifteen, having lost his wife to cancer in the previous year. As a very senior, experienced diplomat, he could have gotten a much more prestigious ambassadorship, but his choice was this professionally quiet assignment in a little Mediterranean backwater. He hoped this would give him and his children the opportunity to recover from the trauma of his wife's suffering and death. Instead, he found himself at the epicenter of a political and military maelstrom that required that he order his own children, along with the families of his American staff, out of this danger zone to our designated safe haven in Beirut, Lebanon. Ironically, Lebanon was in the early throes of its own civil war and was hardly safe.

Most of us had seen a very human side of Ambassador Davies during the period after the Cyprus coup and the Turkish invasion, which required everyone to take all-night communication duty in the front office.

The ambassador, dressed in pajamas, robe, and bedroom slippers, would come padding in to the duty desk during the wee hours and invite us to his adjoining residence for a cup of cocoa and quiet conversation. When our replacements came, he offered the tired officer going off duty to use his guest room instead of going home through the darkened city. The next morning we found bread, cheese, and a pile of fresh oranges to squeeze for juice. His thoughtfulness and caring—for his children and his staff—were obvious.

On August 21, 1974, Secretary of State Henry Kissinger delivered remarks to honor Ambassador Davies. He said, as I paraphrase:

> Rodger Davies embodied the qualities and spirit which mark an American. He chose an unusual profession, a profession which required that to serve his country he leave his home, but he never forgot it.
>
> Wherever he went, the heritage of America was in his heart. He remembered the dignity of the individual where individuals had lost their dignity. He remembered liberty and justice where those rights were under attack. He remembered peace where there was war. In that sense, Rodger Davies never left home.

Postscript: It was at this early point in my career that I began to wonder whether I wanted to continue in the foreign service. I'd been in only one post before, and there had been no physical or emotional danger. These days American diplomats from ambassadors on down are in danger of being killed, intentionally or simply because they got in the way of a wildly fired bullet or an exploding vehicle. But the targeted assassination of Ambassador Davies was highly unusual, and it made me consider the need to rethink my career plans.

CHAPTER 11

Riots: an Almost Daily "Entertainment"

I didn't keep track at the time, but the riots at the embassy after Ambassador Davies' assassination seemed never to end. They had a fairly consistent pattern, which made them no less nerve-racking.

First, our security officer got very little help from the Greek Cypriot police in the way of warning that a mob was headed our way.

Second, the only place for rioters to gather was near the front door, an area fifteen feet wide, sandwiched between a row of tall thorny bushes and a spiked iron fence. If by some chance demonstrators managed to get into this space, they were sitting ducks for tear gas fired from the roof. Since the demonstrators never brought ladders or vehicles with chains to pull down the fence or clear the thorny bushes, and since at least one Marine was always on the roof with tear gas, we usually didn't have to worry about attacks from the front of the building, and the crowd had to content itself with burning the vehicles parked there.

Therefore, the most likely spot from which to expect an attack was the rear entrance to the building. But would-be heroes (mostly older teenagers and adults with nothing better to do) first had to get over another spiked iron fence covered with coils of razor wire. If anyone had thought about it, this could have easily been cut with a special set of wire cutters. Another way of getting over the razor wire required a heavy leather jacket and leather chaps, which most people didn't own (there not being many cowboys on Cyprus). But some always managed to make it into a small inner courtyard near the embassy's heavy wooden back door, further blocked by a barred steel gate, which could be locked on the inside.

The most effective deterrent was the embassy's contingent of eight trained Marine security guards. These young men were all volunteers for this kind of duty but were heavily screened by their officers to ensure they had the discipline to be pleasant to civilians yet be prepared to take antiriot action quickly and as non-lethally as possible.

As the riots came more and more frequently, most of the Marines were usually posted on the roof, busily firing tear gas canisters down on the attackers at any point they tried to get over the fence, barbed wire, or steel gate. The only weakness was that the Marines needed a constant flow of crates of gas canisters, since they couldn't shoot and keep up their gas supplies at the same time. That's where we non-shooting foreign service officers came in, answering Marine radio calls for more gas, stored in the basement and now carried three stories up to the flat roof. Fortunately, we had plenty of water and energy bars since the riots could go on for up to an hour, and everyone needed water and nutrition to keep up the defensive effort.

The oddest thing I remember is how quiet things seemed to remain inside the embassy building. We did not hear the shotguns firing tear gas from the roof or the exhortations and shouting of the crowds gathered around the entrances. The noise simply didn't get through the walls.

All of our support to the Marines seemed to be going well until one of their radios stopped working, and he ran out of tear gas. This allowed the rioters to make it unimpeded into the courtyard and focus on the single steel-barred gate—the only thing that protected us from being invaded. And it soon became obvious that at least two of the rioters were carrying long steel crowbars.

The single Marine on duty in the inner entrance/reception area realized that there was nothing to stop the rioters if they managed to pry the steel-barred gate from its hinges; the wooden inside door would hold only a few minutes. His radio wasn't working, but, fortunately, our security officer, Mark, happened to be with the Marine in the entrance area. They heard one of the guys outside with a crowbar scraping on the steel gate, fishing for an opening and an angle to rip the hinges off the gate's wooden supports, and shouting for others to join him.

It's always amazed me how, in the heat of violence, one can come up with a rational plan of action. Mark was armed only with a shotgun, and there was no gas canister launcher to attach to the gun. He couldn't let these guys get through this barrier, so in seconds he made his decision and barked an order. He and the Marine put on their gas masks. Mark then radioed those of us upstairs to bring down as many cases of gas as we could manage in one trip and grab a gas mask before we came. And—needless to say—hurry!

Four of us got the message and ran to follow his orders. Within ten minutes we four (myself, Mark, and two Marines from the roof, where there was no action at that moment), had made it to the main reception desk in the small room that served both the back and front doors.

"Get your masks on!" Mark calmly ordered. "If you haven't worn one before, get someone to help you adjust it well around your mouth, nose, and eyes. When you're ready, come stand by the cases of gas that you just brought down. *Now*, please!"

I seemed to be the only one having trouble adjusting my one-size–fits-all rubber mask; none of us had had time to practice the art of wearing riot gear since the coup and Ambassador Davies' death. Now I wasn't sure I had it on correctly and went to a fellow FSO for help. He, as ignorant about this as I, did his best to get the thing on so it seemed to fit tightly in the right places. "Okay," I thought to calm my nervousness. "I'm ready. Bring 'em on!" But I had no idea what that meant, Mark not having had the time to explain what he intended.

Finally he shouted quickly, "At least one guy is working on the steel gate with a crowbar to pry it loose. If he succeeds, we're toast. I'm going to ask you to flood this whole area with gas—you've seen the Marines do this when they're throwing the canisters down into the courtyard. If any of them get through, they'll hopefully find it worse inside than outside, and we'll be able to get some repairs made to the steel gate before we go upstairs and have a light dinner with a big dessert.

"Remember, these are not like hand grenades—there's no five-second delay before they go off. And they don't explode: the gas just comes out under compression from one end of the canister. Be sure you're not aiming the canister at anyone; you're not going to play John Wayne—you'll only douse one of us with the gas, and the stuff is not pleasant—it can get around the edges of a mask and disable you or soak someone's clothes and make it impossible to be in the same room with that person.

"Then when the inner door is open, John (one of the other Marines) and I are going to toss out a couple of canisters into the faces of anyone close enough to be a threat. You can't work a crowbar with a face full of tear gas."

By now, I was uncontrollably shaking. I was comfortable with guns, having grown up in Texas hunting birds, squirrels, and rabbits, but we didn't hunt rabbits like this when I was a kid. However, I realized that my assignment now was not complex, so I took a couple of deep breaths through the mask to calm down. Everything worked: I could breathe, I could see through the mask's little Plexiglas window, I checked one of the canisters to be sure I knew what to pull and where to aim it. I was ready.

"Okay!" shouted Mark, his voice muffled by his own mask. "We're going to open the inner door."

John stood behind him with a couple of canisters to toss out. We all checked our masks and our "flooding" canisters. Mark quietly slid the inside security bolt on the wooden door and jerked it open.

Suddenly we were aware of the howling crowd noise outside and the one man with the crowbar working at the steel gate hinges. Mark shouted back to the rest of us, "Flood the place!" at the same time that John opened and tossed the canisters through the bars into the little knot of men working on the gate. I pulled the pin on my canister, carefully aiming it at no one. But then the good plan hit a snag; one of the FSOs, who shall remain nameless, forgot that he had no five-second delay and pulled the pin before checking where it was aiming. The gas shot onto one of the other FSOs, who immediately fell to the floor, rolling wildly in blind agony, unaware that he was now a cloud of gas contaminating everything he touched, which included me. If it had been a scene in a movie, it would have been a Buster Keaton comedy. The trouble was that things were too serious to be funny.

While the other two Marines helped the FSO who'd been hit and tried to get him out of the area, John tossed the gas canister into the small group of rioters at the outer door. Mark and John saw the rioters at the gate fall back from the gas, screaming. However, one of them somehow had the presence of mind to shout back into the crowd for other men to come take his place.

At this point, things got uncomfortable for me. The gas had gotten on me, even if secondarily, and unlike the Hollywood versions of gas masks, mine was obviously leaking. The room was cloudy with the stuff, but the other FSOs apparently could still function, since they continued to open canisters and flood the place. It was like the London fog in that small room.

Mark and John had more serious things to worry about. Another rioter with a crowbar had worked his way up to the steel gate and now, with the wooden door open, was working assiduously on one of the hinges that looked to be the loosest. And he was making progress. John grabbed Mark's shotgun from the floor where he had laid it, and the two of them faced a major decision: they could shoot the rioter, thereby creating a martyr and likely turning the crowd into a truly vicious mob, or they could hope the hinge held. They didn't have enough gas left to repeat the gassing of the group at the gate.

When I later went over that moment in my mind, I realized that their Marine training had kicked in even though they were as scared as the rest of us. They kept their heads and didn't shoot. One of the Marines pulled his riot truncheon out of his belt holder, got a nod from Mark, and waited for the guy with the crowbar to move the bar out of the way, exposing his arm. Then he brought the truncheon down hard and straight on the lower point of the man's arm, likely breaking one or more of the bones in the arm.

The man screamed from both the shock and the solid blow. He fled screaming, scattering those around him. Mark quickly slammed the wooden door and bolted it, then—again calmly—spoke on his radio, asking staff to bring more gas down to the first floor landing, having first wrapped wet rags around their faces. He sent one of the other Marines to switch the air conditioner to the "exhaust" position to pull some of the contaminated air out of the room. Then he came over to me and adjusted my mask so I was not inhaling quite so much gas with the air I needed to function.

He walked over to the adjoining room, where the FSO who had taken the full dose of the canister was, and asked a couple of other FSOs to get him upstairs and have him undress and shower down with plenty of body shampoo. It would help, but he wouldn't be free of the contamination effects until he was thoroughly clean with new clothes.

After the stress of the past few hours, we had to find a bottle of wine to celebrate our victory. We did find the wine, but while the first glass was being poured, the Marine at the reception desk called me on his radio to say there was a telephone call for me. We'd been on and off telephone service for so long, it took a few moments for me to absorb that I was indeed wanted by someone on the phone. Rather than take a chance on losing the call, I hurried down the stairs to the reception area. The exhaust on the air conditioners had worked pretty well, but the rugs, curtains, and furniture still had a strong remainder of gas, which made its way through my gas mask. The Marine handed the phone to me saying, "He says he's from CBS News, and they've heard we had a riot. They want more details about what happened, possible injuries, etc. You're the public affairs officer and spokesman for the embassy—I assume you're the one to take it."

"Yeah, you're right. We'd both be in trouble if you responded to them," I replied through a series of coughs.

There was nothing unexpected about the questions, and they weren't interested in answering my query—cough, cough— about how they'd found out about it so quickly.

"No, no serious injuries to those of us inside (cough, cough.). I can't speak for the rioters except to say a couple of them hollered but got up and ran off, so I have to assume they were not seriously injured. No, no—no more to report at this point (cough, cough). No, I'm not injured, just having a hard time getting the tear gas out of my lungs. No, I don't think it's serious" (I hoped—no one had mentioned getting lung cancer from inhaling tear gas). "Thank you, and if you come up with more questions, please call the State Department spokesman in Washington. We'll be reporting any further details to them." I paused, thinking they were going to say, "Thanks, and good luck." But they had one final question: "Do you happen to have the State Department phone number?"

"No. I assume you've got a telephone book—please use it."

Wild events sometimes pass with prosaic endings. I learned later that someone on night duty in the State Department's 24/7 monitoring room had learned of the riot from my report to CBS—no one else in the embassy had had the time to sit down at a typewriter and get off a cable to Washington. A couple of friends in the United States had heard my international coughing and were kind enough to write a letter with newspaper reports in it about the interview, but my fame—like life—was fleeting.

CHAPTER 12

Flying the Friendly Foreign Service Skies

When I first joined the foreign service, I had not flown much, even in the United States. Prices were high, and airplane food, especially in economy class, was considered as tasty as warmed-over school lunches. But hope sprang eternal, and I envisioned myself dressed in a suit and tie, sipping martinis with beautiful stewardesses. In fact, while it didn't quite meet my fantasies, flying the commercial "friendly skies" in the mid-1960s wasn't all that bad. One could buy a martini if one wished or a small bottle of wine, and before computers learned to cram as many bodies as possible into medieval torture seats, one could end up in a row of three seats with two of them empty, and thus enjoy the luxury of stretching out with feet elevated for long trips.

That kind of flying for me ended abruptly with the Greek Cypriot coup and subsequent Turkish invasion in 1974. Cyprus' international airport was bombed by Turkish fighters to prevent the Greeks from resupplying their troops. Passenger aircraft on the ground were either destroyed in the bombing or rendered useless by gaping holes in the runway. Anyone wishing to travel to or from Cyprus had to come by ship from Athens—a thirty-six-hour journey, which was not up to cruise ship standards.

There was, however, one way to fly to and from Cyprus. The British owned sovereign rights to a small air base on the southeastern end of the island and let the diplomatic American community use it for official travel. The base had other uses too: it served as an eastern Mediterranean landing point for British and American surveillance flights over whatever countries were deemed worth watching.

American families and nonessential personnel had been evacuated just after the Turkish invasion. Of the two Greek speakers, one was allowed to leave with his wife, who was having a troublesome pregnancy, leaving me to handle alone the large numbers of American journalists who descended on the island with their camera crews after the riots began. My second wife, Tamara, was evacuated to the Netherlands, but I was designated as essential and therefore stayed behind.

The evacuation had been expected to last only a brief time, but as it dragged on, all of us remaining began to look for a way to become nonessential for a few days and fly to Europe to visit wives and children. Thank goodness, due to the cooperation of the British, we were allowed to take one of the daily planes out of the British base to England, where we could catch European flights to our families' locations. I was lucky to get five days' leave, which meant five days of companionship, good food, and Dutch courtesy.

Near the end of my Dutch holiday, we got word that wives without children could return to Cyprus. Families with children had to enroll them in European schools because the schools in Cyprus had not yet reopened. So my wife, Tamara, and I caught a flight to England and then a British military plane to Athens. We learned that there were two Greek American congressmen stuck in Athens, and, rather than take the slow ship to Cyprus, our Athens embassy had offered to fly them to Cyprus using an embassy military aircraft. We would therefore accompany the congressmen and offer any briefings they wanted.

So we flew into Athens, spent one night at a hotel, and reported to the airport at ten the following morning. There we discovered that our aircraft was an old World War II DC-6, a two-engine prop job that had been converted to transport a dozen passengers as well as cargo. A single air force sergeant, Fred Olson, made up the cabin crew. He was already on the tarmac awaiting us and showed us to our seats, one row having been removed and a second turned around to accommodate a small briefing table.

The congressmen finally showed up, looking somewhat the worse for wear after a night of cocktails and dinner during which the Greeks assured them how terrible the Turks had been to invade Cyprus, emphasizing that "brutal" Turkish troops had driven young children away from their parents to "prison camps." Both congressmen, a senator and a representative, were of Greek ancestry. As they boarded our aircraft, you could see from their glances that they were not impressed. Compared to first-class commercial aircraft, this was indeed a step down. I introduced myself and Tamara as well as Sergeant Olson. Fred had done this gig before and knew how to make a better first impression than the worn seats and scratched windows of a twenty-five-year-old airplane.

"Welcome, gentlemen, to luxury itself! As you can see, we have rearranged the furniture so that you can actually look each other in the eye while enjoying conversation during our two-hour run to the wonderful island of Cyprus—that is, if both engines perform at their usual fifty percent efficiency. We are fully fueled and ready to go as soon as I complete my regulation safety instructions.

"First, allow me to emphasize that your seat belts are there to be buckled, and since you have seen this demonstrated several hundred times, I'll assume you know how to insert the buckle until it clicks and then pull the belt snuggly around your waist.

"Please note the exits on this fine aircraft. The door you came in is one of them; another is in the rear of the aircraft. There was originally a large ramped door out of which cargo could be pushed with parachutes attached, but it is now blocked by cases of booze, American sliced bread, and jars of peanut butter, for which our fine diplomatic colleagues in Cyprus will pay before we let them unload it. So that exit is not available. There are three World War II parachutes somewhere back there, but to my knowledge they have not been tested since the aircraft rolled off the assembly line. The same is true for the life vests under your seat, so I will not make any guesses on their viability.

"There is a small hatch forward in the cockpit, but it has to accommodate two overweight pilots and one skinny sergeant, so please don't assume you will be able to get out that way in a hurry.

"Lastly, under the fine carpeting covering this main center aisle there is a fourth way out, but please note that you must roll up the carpet in order to reach the levers that will open this small hatch. That wasn't so complicated, was it? That's one advantage of aging cargo aircraft: they can't make them with too many emergency exits that won't be blocked by the cases of cargo they were designed to carry."

My wife and I thought Sergeant Olson's presentation was as humorously informative as he intended, but the congressmen merely looked like they had hangovers, which they did.

Fred disappeared for a moment and returned with a jar of peanuts and four cans of warm Coke, apologizing that the smoked salmon would not be ready until the prop engines had warmed up enough to emit their usual cloud of petroleum-flavored smoke.

Worried now that Fred might be going a little over the top and could wake up the next morning demoted to corporal, I told the congressmen briefly why we were on their flight and that I'd be glad to give them any briefing on Cyprus they wished.

"Look, Mr. Grimland," snapped the representative, "we were up until two this morning, and we're exhausted. We'll give you five minutes, and then we'd like to catch some sleep."

"All right, Congressman. What is your primary purpose for coming to Cyprus? Let me address any points I can make to that."

"Look, fella," said the representative, "We both have large Greek American constituencies in our districts. We want to have our pictures taken in some Greek Cypriot refugee camps—plenty of starving kids would be great. You just arrange the photographer; we'll kiss the babies and pass out some candy, okay?"

So this was simply a campaign boondoggle. The guy seemed not to care one whit about how the Greek Cypriots got themselves into this mess. He just wanted some photos for next year's campaign to show his constituents that he was taking care of anything with the label "Greek" on it. Finished with delivering his message, he grabbed a small pillow, put on a sleeping mask, and passed out.

The senator seemed a little more apologetic "Excuse my friend here—it was indeed a late night. I am interested in whether the Turks used American-supplied NATO arms in their invasion. What do you know of that?"

"Senator, I know you'll be speaking with our acting ambassador about this, so nothing I can tell you would be anything but my personal, off-the-record opinion. You want hard facts that I don't have."

"Well, I'd like your opinion, Mr. Grimland. And it will stay off the record. But I find it's useful to know people's feelings as well as the facts, if you don't mind."

"Well, Senator. I've watched the Greeks and Greek Cypriots dig themselves into this hole for four years now. A relatively small number of Greek Cypriots want political union with Greece, but a minority—urged on by the current mainland Greek government—pushed this in the press and in the Greek-officered National Guard. They saw Cypriot President and Archbishop Makarios as an obstacle to this plan and tried to get rid of him, naming in his place a Greek Cypriot thug named Nikos Samson, who has the deserved reputation of slaughtering Turkish Cypriots whenever he thinks he can get away with it. When he was named president, nothing could stop the mainland Turks from using military equipment from wherever they could get it to go in and protect the Turkish Cypriot minority on the island. Greek troops also had NATO-supplied weapons, and I don't doubt that they used them against each other as well as the invading Turks. So everyone is to blame, including the United States for supplying both these long-standing enemies with the means to go to war with each other."

The senator nodded, not indicating he agreed with me but rather that he heard me. "Thank you, Mr. Grimland. I appreciate your personal honesty. Now I think I'll grab a few winks myself, if you don't mind."

The plane droned on. I could feel it laboring against a headwind from the east but didn't think much about it. Our two engines seemed to have no trouble keeping up.

About an hour later, we began our descent to the British base, and as we got lower, I could see whitecaps on the surface of the water. We made a wide swing to the south and approached the runway. Now the headwind became a crosswind from the east. We came down slowly, close enough to see that indeed the whitecaps were much more than light spray. Sergeant Fred came by and folded up the table between the congressmen and my wife and me, then buckled himself securely into a seat near the front of the aircraft. Tamara and I sat facing backward on the left side of the plane just behind the wing. I woke both congressmen and suggested they prepare for a possibly rough landing. No one argued.

Slowly the plane eased down until the wheels touched the runway. But the pilot, sensing something, gunned the engines, and we took to the air again. Fred got up from his seat and opened the cockpit door, then shouted over the roar of the engines, "Got a pretty rough crosswind down here, folks— almost too much to land in. We're going to come back for a second try since our secondary landing spot is Israel, and there's no telling when we'd be able to get the congressmen back here for another try."

The plane climbed back up and circled the field again. As I looked down, I could see a British air/sea rescue helicopter being rolled out of its hangar, and a couple of fire trucks right behind it.

Again we made our approach, again the wheels touched the runway, and I thought we'd made it. But suddenly, a strong wind shear from the east hit us. I saw the left wing dip, scraping the runway and breaking off the last two thirds but leaving the engine attached and running. As we careened down the runway I heard the pilot gunning the engines. "My god," I thought, "he doesn't know he's lost a wing, and he's trying to take off again." Not thinking, I reached for my seat buckle to get up and tell the pilot something idiotic like, "Excuse me, sir, but did you know we've lost the left wing?" Tamara jerked my hand back from my buckle, a panicked reaction that brought me to my senses. But why was he alternately revving up the engines?

I learned later that this was exactly what he should have done. By alternately gunning the engines, he kept control of the now unbalanced and wounded plane and kept it from spinning around and possibly breaking up. That would have caused fuel to spill all over the runway, which could then be ignited by a spark from metal scraping the asphalt, possibly blowing up the plane.

As we careened down the runway, I heard Fred over the din of noise shouting, "Hold on! We're going to crash into the barrier!" An earthen berm at the end of the runway was designed to do just that: stop an uncontrolled plane from running off the end of the runway and plunging into the sea. We plowed into it at a pretty good clip; fortunately, we all were securely buckled in, as was the whiskey, peanut butter, and white bread.

No sooner had we come to a stop than Fred jumped up and ripped the carpet off the floor, exposing the floor escape hatch. "We've got to get out of here; we've still got fuel on board and there's fire danger," he shouted.

Jerking the hatch open, he grabbed Tamara and dropped her neatly through the hole, about five feet from the ground. The representative was already up and needed no encouragement. I was now the farthest from the hatch, but the senator was down on his knees pawing around on the floor underneath his seat, saying, "I've got to get my briefcase; I've got to get my briefcase!"

This was not the time for an argument that he couldn't absorb. Reaching down, I grabbed his belt and pulled him into the aisle, then grabbed his coat collar, dragged him a couple of steps, and shoved him out of the hatch. I followed, and then Fred jumped as soon as I was out of the way. Picking ourselves up, we all ran away as fast as we could, just as the fire trucks rolled up and began to foam down the plane and ground. We watched for a minute or so until we felt the wash from the air/sea rescue helicopters behind us. A couple of men jumped from the choppers with blankets and began throwing them around us. "It's all right, luv, it's all right!" they shouted to Tamara while rushing us to the chopper, its rotors still cutting the air. We all piled in. Our pilots had come out of the small hatch in the cockpit, but they stood beside the fire trucks in case help was needed.

Our helicopter took off, getting us as far away as possible from a potential explosion. It was only a five-minute flight back to the receiving center, where, in true British fashion, hot cups of tea were handed out. A doctor confirmed that everyone was shaken but not injured. The two congressmen sat sipping their tea, a British officer nearby. I went over to them and tried to chat, but nothing sensible would come. Our acting ambassador had come down to meet the congressmen and take them back to Nicosia, so I happily turned them over to him. Tamara was okay and preferred to wait with me for my car. I went over to the British officer to thank him. "Whew, Colonel, that was some wind out there. Do you lose many planes on days like this?"

"Not really," he replied. And smiling mischievously, he added, "Actually, we don't have Americans landing here very often."

Postscript: It's ironic that I would later survive without harm one other near-crash in India and that this first close call happened on one of our own American aircraft and was due only to a fluke in the wind. The pilots reacted coolly and professionally, the vintage aircraft held up in spite of its age, and we delivered whiskey and white bread to our deprived colleagues in Cyprus.

But the incident left a sour taste in my mouth, mainly from the representative's manner and blatantly political reason for demanding the trip. The senator, on the other hand, may have had a similar underlying campaign agenda, but he seemed genuinely interested in getting the facts of the situation on Cyprus rather than accepting the unquestioning assumptions of his ethnic American voters. Our democratic system produces both types of political leaders.

CHAPTER 13

A Continuing Journey to Ithaka

I walked out of the US Embassy in Nicosia in the summer of 1975, a thirty-one-year-old foreign service officer. Quickly but carefully, I scanned the area around the outer gate, a habit acquired during the violence of the past year. I was tired and tense.

I had just finished a round of farewell calls on those still left after the previous turbulent year in Cyprus. In spite of new drapes and industrial carpeting in the embassy's reception area, the building still had the acrid smell of tear gas fired a year before by the Marine security guards as rioters attempted to overrun the embassy. I had now done my diplomatic duty, calling on the ambassador, with whom I had experienced several angry professional disagreements. The ambassador had merely smiled tightly and wished me well, visibly relieved to be rid of me.

A car waited to take me to the British air base on the southern coast of the island. It was still the only way off the island by air, the international airport in Nicosia remaining closed after the Turkish invasion.

I glanced at the embassy parking lot, scarred with burn marks where rioters had torched a dozen vehicles. A new Marine guard watched over the scene from a rooftop observation post, armed with a tear gas launcher and a studied look of indifference. "I hope he never has to go through what his comrades endured," I said to myself, remembering how the previous Marine detachment had saved many lives.

The drive to the British base was hot but uneventful. As we pulled up to the nondescript departure lounge, a crew readied the twenty-seat British Viscount turboprop. An RAF sergeant emerged from the plane and came into the building:

"Ready, sir? You're the only passenger today, so you'll have your choice of seats. We can board anytime."

"Let's go, Sergeant. I'm more than ready to leave."

I settled into my seat just as the plane's engines coughed to life. "At last; I've never been so glad to get out of any place."

Two hours later, the Viscount touched down in Athens. Finding my way to the TWA ticket counter, I handed my papers to a young agent. The perky young woman chirped, "Oh, Cyprus! Have you been on holiday? They say the beaches are wonderful! Where are you going today?"

I was on the verge of major burnout and needed time and space to think about whether to return to the diplomatic service. Not only had I just survived the turmoil of recent events in Cyprus, but my personal life had also experienced a great deal of upheaval.

My first wife and I had separated early in my Cyprus tour; she had returned to the United States with our infant daughter. Other stressful episodes followed, some of them on the island and others on trips away. By the time I left the island in 1975 for my two-year leave of absence, I had re-married, and my new wife was able to get a teaching job as conductor and director of music programs at the Quaker-founded colleges in Haverford and Bryn Mawr.

So in August of 1975 I flew into Philadelphia and made my way to a rented house near Haverford. I first enjoyed having the time to read the *New York Times* from cover to cover in the morning. Then I built a photo processing darkroom in our basement and delighted in spending entire days learning to print black and white photos I'd taken.

Feeling the need to deepen my intellectual exposure to Western philosophy, I enrolled at Haverford in a course on basic Western philosophy. Drawn to mystical interests, I tried some programs at a nearby Quaker center for study and contemplation and decided to spend six months as a resident student at Pendle Hill.

At Pendle Hill, in addition to courses on mysticism, I explored the arts, especially clay and creative movement. I was fortunate to have John Yungblut as my mentor and teacher. John introduced me to Quaker thought, and I participated in Pendle Hill's Quaker services. The silence of Quaker meetings had a strong and lasting appeal, and I continued to seek out Quaker meetings wherever I went in later years. I am now a member of the Billings Friends' Meeting.

All these separate threads of the Pendle Hill experience helped heal me after the violence of Cyprus. After six months in that very special place, I fitted out a truck as a single camper and took to the highways of the western United States for two months. Finishing in Washington, DC, I was finally ready to resume my career in the foreign service.

The road and journey changed; another door was about to open.

TURKEY

CHAPTER 14

Misadventures in Istanbul

(This is slightly out of chronological order, but since it takes place in Turkey, I have included it with other stories from Turkey.)

In the 1970s when I was posted in Cyprus, I began working with an American woman who was a professor of music at the State University of New York (SUNY) at Albany. We were interested in bringing American musicians to Cyprus for a summer of symphonic and choral concerts. When we finished our organizing, some forty young American musicians as well as a few bigger names, all of whom paid their own way out to Cyprus for nineteen concerts in three weeks, made the Summer '72 Festival a reality.

When the festival was over Tamara, the music professor, and I married. Not content to play the typical role of a foreign service wife, she began to look for musical opportunities in neighboring countries.

The closest was an offer by the Istanbul Symphony for a guest conductor gig—a couple of concerts in that amazing city. She jumped at the chance, and together we flew to Istanbul.

The concerts she conducted were well-received. After the final one, a distinguished older gentleman and his wife visited the green room to offer their congratulations. Introducing himself as the Austrian Consulate's cultural attaché, he and his wife invited us to dinner the following evening at their home. It was to be a casual little affair; a small Viennese chamber group was in town, and they had invited a few friends for dinner and music.

We accepted, having no idea what "a casual little affair" would entail. As Tamara's concert dress was dirty from her performance, she chose the only other dress she brought: a brightly flowered, loose garment. I had brought only a tan camel's hair sport coat and one tie, since I was there in no official capacity. Dressed in our limited finery, we caught a taxi to the address we'd been given.

We found the apartment in what appeared to be an upscale neighborhood of Istanbul. As we got off the elevator and walked over to ring the doorbell, we noticed a green velvet-covered seating chart on the wall listing the names of the guests. A quick look was disconcerting: Tamara's name card was placed to the host's right, mine to the hostess' right, and more than twenty other cards were around what was obviously a very long, formal dinner table. My stomach flipped; this was "a casual little dinner with a few friends?"

The door was opened not by the host but by a servant in uniform, who escorted us into the assembled group. The Viennese chamber strings, with the musicians in tuxedos, played some light Mozart in one corner, and, in the dim light, we saw the other guests, all dressed in basic black and diamonds. Tamara in her brightly flowered dress and I in my camel's hair coat were the only ones that fit my Texas definition of "casual."

Our host appeared and began to take us around the room, introducing us to ... the last princess of the Ottoman Empire and her Turkish businessman fiancé ... the visiting *Time* magazine correspondent and his wealthy-looking partner for the evening, in black and diamonds, of course ... a foreign military attaché in dress uniform with full medals and his distinctly uncasual wife.

I hadn't been in the diplomatic service very long and didn't remember any of my training instructions about what to do when dropped through a rabbit hole into a *very* unfamiliar dimension. So to calm my jangled nerves, when the first liveried servant came by with a drink tray and caviar, I ignored the caviar and immediately grabbed what looked like the most potent alcoholic beverage, which turned out to be vodka. I was not a heavy drinker, but I needed a strong shot of confidence.

I remember nothing of the cocktail conversation. Between the Mozart, the black dresses and tuxedos, the diamonds, and trying to remember a few names—"Oh, you don't have to call me 'your Highness'"—I quickly found that as soon as my glass was empty, a waiter refilled it. Gradually, of course, I calmed down. It took a few glasses of vodka, but I could feel my confidence come back to where I could assume the outward trappings of a knowledgeable diplomat.

After being introduced to the Ottoman princess, Tamara was deftly whisked away to be shown off to other guests, and I contented myself with the visiting *Time* correspondent. "Why the hell does he travel with a tux in his suitcase?" I thought.

In time, a servant rang the dinner chime, and we filed in to our assigned seats. I practically needed a telescope to see Tamara at the other end of the long table, before noticing an array of implements carefully laid out to the left, right, and above my plate. Each place setting also included large crystal glasses for water and two smaller ones for white and red wine.

Just as I realized that I would have to watch my hostess carefully as to which cutlery to use when, she engaged me in conversation. I'm sure her questions about Cyprus and my work were more planned and coherent than my responses, but the first flush of vodka confidence was wearing thin. About that time, the waiters began the dinner service—soup, followed by a fish course, followed by meat—and, thank goodness, white and red wine to match each course.

The wine glasses were small, but every time I emptied one, it was immediately refilled by an efficient servant.

This was definitely not Texas, I realized—no macaroni and cheese at home in familiar surroundings. But I quickly found that the wine eased my sense of discomfort almost as effectively as the vodka, especially since I already had a good start with the vodka. I began to respond to questions and comments with increasing vitality and verve.

Because the table was so large, and the guest on my left was working hard to engage the princess, I spoke mainly with my hostess as we made our way through the various courses. By the time the main course was served, the waiters had switched to red wine, which has always affected me more than white. I was now convinced that I was the most interesting guest at the table, and so my stories became louder and certainly wittier. I felt that I was on my way to an ambassadorship.

As we finished the second to last course, salad, I was truly in my element and didn't notice that the dessert waiter was coming up on my side with a large crystal bowl of chocolate mousse. Even if I had seen him, I couldn't miss the denouement of the story I was telling that required raising my arms and pointing at the ceiling. Thanks partially to what happened next, I have no idea what striking point I was in the process of making or why it necessitated bringing my right arm down suddenly and sharply. But I did so just as the waiter preparing to serve me from the bowl of chocolate mousse had positioned it under my elbow. *Down* came my camel's-hair-clad elbow, with vigor, into the crystal bowl.

No one at the far end of the table deigned to notice. In an effort to save her guest's dignity, the hostess gave the waiter a look that could kill and said quietly, "Oh, you fool!"

Again, my memory gets hazy after my elbow went into the bowl. But the bowl was whisked away, and two waiters divested me of my coat, which disappeared. The hostess resumed her conversation. No remarks were made; others who had obviously witnessed my *faux pas* looked away or quickly returned to conversation with the guest next to them. A fresh bowl of mousse appeared, the dessert was served uneventfully to those who hadn't received it, and suddenly utterly sober, I followed their cue and ate my mousse, quiet and chastened. I gave up on my fantasy of getting an ambassadorship.

Coffee appeared, and the now cautious waiters asked if I wanted any. I accepted, hoping to sit for a while before having to get up and possibly knock something over.

We lingered for perhaps twenty minutes while the chamber players struck up a little more sedate music for digestion. I began to wonder how or when I was going to get my sport coat back, when suddenly a waiter appeared with it. Slipping my arm into the sleeve, which had recently been dripping with chocolate mousse, I noticed that the sleeve was clean! Not a spot of chocolate marred it. To this day I don't know what was done to that coat: the sleeve wasn't wet; it was indeed the coat I wore coming in (the American store label was intact). There was no way they could have rousted a Turkish tailor at that hour to whip out a new coat in twenty minutes. It shall always remain one of life's major mysteries, at least to me.

People began to take their leave. The Austrian attaché came with Tamara from the other end of the table to tell me how much he'd enjoyed having us as guests, and ... and ... and ... he'd have his own car take us back to the hotel.

Thoroughly sober now I responded as pleasantly as I could and made my way with Tamara to the door, where a servant helped us into the elevator and then into the car.

"What happened?" asked Tamara as we were driven back to the hotel. "I was talking and looking the other way, but there seemed to be a mild commotion at your end of the table."

"You don't want to know," I responded. "Not tonight. I'll tell you about it in the morning."

"Okay. But don't forget."

"No ... I won't forget. Ever!"

CHAPTER 15

Finding Farouk

The phone call from Washington came in shortly after midnight.

At the time (in the early 1980s), I was our consulate general's public affairs officer in Istanbul. Having just left Washington doing a job I greatly enjoyed, I still found enough in the exotic city of Istanbul to keep me busy. I liked the Turks, their food and their manners: when they toasted each other, they didn't clink glasses to each other's health or prosperity but rather "Şerife!" (To honor!)

I was surprised when the phone rang late that night; usually Washington called my supervisor in Ankara, who relayed anything urgent to me.

The voice on the other end greeted me by name.

"Hey, Dave. How are things in Istanbul?"

"Fine, Gordon. But don't you have clocks all over the Voice of America to tell you what time it is here in Istanbul?" I'd met Gordon before and knew he was doing a tour with VOA's office in Washington, but I didn't know precisely what his assignment was.

"Uh, yeah. I guess we do, but I'm not in a studio, so I never look at 'em."

"Well, I'm awake now, Gordon. It's a little after midnight here, so what's going on in VOA?

"Dave, I'm the head of the Iranian language service. Great career move for someone who doesn't speak Farsi and has no desire to be posted to Tehran. But I've got a bunch of Iranian expats working for me in my division, and one of them is a guy with a problem. I was hoping you could help."

All I knew about Iran at that point was that the Iran-Iraq War was in full swing, having begun in 1980. (It would go on with horrible loss of life until 1984.) The media were covering the fact that our Reagan-led government was aiding the Iraqis, the aggressors who first invaded Iran, in their attempt to take over the country in the midst of Ayatollah Khomeini's revolution. Our desire to get revenge on Khomeini had made us bedfellows with Saddam Hussein.

I'd read newspaper reports of the United States shipping mustard gas to Saddam, some of which he was using on the Iranians and some he was holding in case his own Shiite subjects in Iraq decided to be a fifth column for their Shiite brothers in Iran. The trouble was that the gas was manufactured in Virginia and shipped in containers clearly marked with the name of the American company producing the gas. So obviously the Iranians weren't kindly disposed toward us Americans.

I waited to learn how I could help him with his problem. I didn't envy Gordon his job of overseeing Iranians hired to "tell America's story" to Iran.

Gordon continued: "Well, the head Iranian in our Farsi language service is getting a divorce from his wife. He's in America, of course, and she's in Tehran."

"So how do I come in?" I had enough trouble handling my own marriage without playing counselor to a couple of Iranians.

Gordon continued. "Well, the couple has a son who just turned eighteen, and you know that the Iranians are throwing every kid they can get into the army, probably to act as human mine detectors and get blown up in the process. So the mother and father have worked together to get the kid out of Iran."

I was beginning to see a dim connection to me, posted in Istanbul, but said nothing.

"The kid's name is Farouk. And like every other parent who can afford to arrange it, his mother is arranging to get their boy to the Turkish border and turn him over to Kurdish smugglers. The Kurds are supposed to get the young man on a bus to a big Turkish city, in this case Istanbul. In return, they get a large sum of cash.

The problem is that it's winter, and the Kurds put these kids on mules and haul them over the mountains along Turkey's border before dumping them at some village bus station. The mother has somehow gotten word that Farouk's feet are badly frostbitten ..."

"And he's in Istanbul, right, Gordon?" I reluctantly concluded.

"Yeah, but we don't know where. These kids—and there are a lot of them—have entered Turkey illegally and tend to hang low in cheap hotels until arrangements can be made to get them fake American passports and refugee visas to the United States."

I hoped Gordon remembered that Turkish Intelligence undoubtedly tapped the telephones of American diplomats, and figured it wouldn't take them long to find one that was helping an Iranian boy in Istanbul. I could only hope that it was so late at night that the telephone eavesdroppers had gone to sleep themselves.

"Gordon, Istanbul is a city of five million people. How the hell am I supposed to locate one sick Iranian teenager in a flophouse?"

"I know, Dave. But the father is worried sick about his son and will do anything to see that he gets medical help. Their network is already working on getting him a false American passport with a Turkish entry stamp in it and a refugee visa to the United States. If you prefer, I'll just tell the father that you tried but couldn't find Farouk."

Although I was not being asked to get the boy an American passport, it would be frowned upon by my American colleagues if I knew the boy was involved in illegally getting one, and I would be given a serious slap on the wrist. And if the Turks knew that I knew of plans to have the passport stamped with a false Turkish entry visa, they might make an objection to my supervisors.

I nevertheless said to Gordon, "I haven't the foggiest idea how to go about this, but let me sleep on it and see if there's anything I can even try. I'll call you back when I know if it's possible and, hopefully, how he is."

I hung up the phone, but there was no sleep to be had as I began to consider how I was going to make an honest attempt to find Farouk. Driving around the cheaper neighborhoods of Istanbul at night shouting "Farouk?" didn't seem like a starter.

Bleary-eyed, I went to my office the next morning. My usual routine was to get a briefing from Bertan, my senior press advisor, about the Turkish papers. In spite of my having waded through nine months of intensive Turkish, Bertan could do a summary job of the dozen major Turkish papers faster than I could get through a single paragraph of the first one.

Bertan came in with his papers and looked mildly surprised when I got up and shut the door behind him. I'd made my decision.

"Bertan, I've got a not-so-small problem, and I need to ask you to hear me out and keep it strictly to yourself."

"Of course, boss," he replied, somewhat relieved that his day might prove more interesting than he'd anticipated.

I related the whole story of Gordon's call and ended saying, "So how do I find a seriously ill Iranian boy in this metropolis?"

Bertan didn't even pause. "First, you have to stay out of it, boss. There is too much for you to lose by anyone even hinting that you're involved. Let me go see some of my Turkish journalist friends who know something about this problem with Iranian kids stuck in Turkey. Even though they'll guess I'm asking on behalf of you, they won't blow your involvement, I'll be sure I talk only to people I trust. And now, don't ask me any questions. If you don't know what's going on, you won't have to lie about it."

"Okay, I understand, and thank you in advance. What do you say we skip the morning press briefing?"

Bertan's blue eyes twinkled. "Sure thing, boss."

"Only one thing, Bertan. I've got to talk to the American doctor who runs the American hospital here in Istanbul. He's been here all his life, and he invented the word *discretion*. If we find Farouk, we'll have to get him to a doctor who can do something and keep quiet about it."

Again, Bertan smiled. "You Americans always think ahead," he chuckled. "I'll bet this boy is already half way to Switzerland by now, and no one here will ever know about it. But if not, you're right. We can't take the chance if he has frost-bitten feet."

And with that half-hopeful observation, he disappeared.

Nothing happened that day. I was dying to ask Bertan what he was learning but recognized his good advice: "Don't ask. You don't have to lie about what you don't know."

The one thing I was able to do was to take a taxi over to the American hospital and spend fifteen minutes with Dr. Winkler (known by all as "Wink"), explaining what we might need. He merely nodded and said, "I understand. If he's found, get the boy to me as soon as you can."

Day two was almost over when Bertan came in and said, "I think you'd better go home a little early this afternoon, boss. You may have an unexpected guest to take care of."

I couldn't believe it but took off about midafternoon and made my way home. Around 5:00 p.m., a Turkish taxi pulled up and two boys got out, one of them helping the other slowly climb the stairs on painful feet to our apartment. He left him at the open door, where I was waiting.

"Farouk?" I asked.

"Yes, sir. I'm supposed to come see you," he said in accented but perfect English.

"I'm Dave Grimland, Farouk. Let me make a phone call to a doctor and see if he's available. He asked to see you right away."

"Yes, sir," he replied, trusting me completely in spite of having just met me.

It took us nearly an hour to reach Wink's office in the evening rush hour traffic, but he immediately took Farouk into an examining room, inviting me to join them. I waited while Wink removed Farouk's shoes and socks and some dirty bandages. He cleaned his feet and had him put them into basins of cool water, changing the cool water gradually to warmer water to get the circulation going. I could tell that one foot was a little better off than the other, but it was obviously an uncomfortable procedure for Farouk. Finally satisfied that there was circulation in both feet, Wink rubbed some antibiotic ointment on the skin and gave Farouk an injection of antibiotics.

"Take him home, Dave. I'll give you some pain pills for him—those feet must be very painful. About the only thing you can do is wait and feed him up. He's young, and kids survive things we oldsters couldn't. Bring him back in tomorrow and let me look at him. But you need to plan on a hungry, sore houseguest for at least a week."

Thankfully, Wink was right. His checkup showed improvement, as did Farouk's appetite. We waited, wondering what was next. I called Gordon and brought him up to date.

"My God, Dave, how'd you do it?"

"Don't ask, Gordon. I'm not even sure myself."

Gordon told me he was going to tell Farouk's father the good news. "Now it's up to him," Gordon said. "He says he's got everything arranged and an operative will show up in a day or two with everything that's needed. And, Dave, thanks so much. Your guys—whoever they are—saved a young man's life."

The next day, a taxi pulled up at our apartment, and a shady-looking Turk speaking Farsi handed Farouk an envelope and disappeared as abruptly as he had come. Farouk showed me the contents of the envelope: a brand new but artificially wrinkled American passport with a Turkish entry stamp and what I assumed was a forged US visa, an airplane ticket to Washington via London for two days later, and a couple of hundred used US dollars. Farouk tried to give me half of it, but I shook my head, "You'll need it more than I," I said, "and I'll see to it that the helpers are thanked on our behalf."

Sure enough a taxi pulled up two days later, and he hobbled down the stairs, giving me a hug at the bottom. "Thank you, sir. Allah will reward you."

"He already has, Farouk: I've had the greatest pleasure in meeting and getting to know you."

***

About a year later, my wife and I left for home leave in the United States. When we arrived in Washington, I had to go to my office for a few days of standard debriefing, and in the manila envelope with my schedule of appointments was a formal invitation from Farouk's father to dinner at his home.

We went, of course, and walked into a room full of obviously wealthy Iranian expatriates and Gordon. As I had assumed, these Iranians didn't let religion get in the way of a good glass of something alcoholic.

Farouk's father tapped his glass of wine, and introduced us in flawless English to the group of Iranians, who applauded his complimentary words. There in the middle of the group was Farouk. He came over and introduced himself, "Hello again, Mr. Grimland, I'm 'Frank:' I work at a local McDonald's. Perhaps you'll let me buy you lunch!"

I smiled. But standing on an exquisite Persian carpet and eating Caspian Sea caviar seemed much preferable at the moment. I raised my glass to "Frank" and his proud father, smiled and said, "*Şerife*, Frank, may Allah bless you and your family and friends."

***

I have had no contact with Farouk since the party at his father's home in Arlington sometime around 1983. And since I can't remember his last name, I doubt that I'll be able to contact him.

My colleague and friend Bertan died a number of years ago, but I did tell him several times how much I appreciated his help in locating Farouk. Dr. Winkler too has passed away. He was a special man, whose nonjudgmental empathy and discretion I could count on in a world so prone to frivolous gossip and half-truths.

And even though I do not know to this day which Turkish journalists helped locate Farouk, I hope they realize how much they did to ensure Farouk's future. They did it for him and as a favor to me. I've learned and relearned over the years that when a Turk accepts you as a *çok ınsan bir adam*—a very "human" person—he holds you as a friend for life. It's a compliment and a commensurate responsibility that I do not take lightly.

CHAPTER 16

"Only One of Us Can Sing, Mr. President ... and I'm the One on Stage"

Some stories are simply too good to die. And in fact, they don't; rather, they enter a society's myth as something larger and more defining than just a story.

When I was assigned as the consulate general's public affairs officer in Istanbul, I quickly sensed that the dozen Turkish staffers I inherited were truly special. Each had his or her own specialty: press specialist, cultural specialist, librarians, secretaries, administrative staffer, etc. They also knew how to work as a team, not a flock of prima donnas. I quickly understood that they were my vital lifeline to the Istanbul community of journalists, educators, artists, and intellectuals, and that I would succeed or fail depending on whether I could learn to lead from behind—and in the process, to listen and learn.

One of these wonderful people was our senior cultural specialist. Meral Selcuk had a special "niceness" quality that we could all use more of. There is no other way to put it: she was simply *pleasant* to everyone from janitors to ambassadors.

Besides working for the American government, she was well-known in her own right as the daughter of Turkey's most famous singer, *Ustad* Munir Nurettin Selcuk. *Ustad* is the Turkish honorific for "master," as in "master violinist" or "master bricklayer." It is equally applicable to both craftsmen and artists. He had a beautiful tenor voice and had introduced old arabesque songs to Turkey.

Ustad Munir presented these "taverna" songs with pride and creativity; he sang in white tie and tux, with a small orchestra of strings supporting him. Turks went crazy for his music. And not only Turks. He sang before the king of Egypt, the shah of Iran, the kings of Jordan—true Middle Eastern royalty. Most unusual was the fact that he allowed his young daughter, Meral, to sing on stage with him. "Nice" Turkish girls did not perform in public in the 1920s and '30s. So Meral grew up in those heretofore forbidden circles. In time she married and had a daughter, and now her grandson works in cancer research and treatment in the United States.

Unfortunately, *Ustad* Munir died a little less than a year after I'd arrived, and since he was not in good health prior to his death, I never met him. At his funeral, huge wreaths from dignitaries all over the Middle East were on display.

Meral was modest about her father's fame, and I had to hear this story about her father from someone else before she confirmed it.

By the time Mustafa Kemal Ataturk succeeded in founding the modern Turkish Republic in 1923, including developing a multiparty political system that elected him its first president, he had already confided to his friends that for Turkey to be a modern republic, it had to be a secular one. So he abolished the caliphate and set up a Ministry of Religious Affairs to control the imams. He set an example of "the modern Turk" in his own lifestyle: he donned a hat instead of the Ottoman *fez*, and encouraged his adopted daughters to make their public mark on Turkish society. He changed the alphabet from Arabic to Roman letters in an amazingly short time for a society that was largely illiterate at the time.

A lover of Western classical music, Ataturk was also first and foremost, a Turk. He loved all things Turkish, including the singing of young Munir Nurettin Selcuk. When Ataturk moved into the Çankaya Presidential Palace in Ankara, he often invited close friends and political associates to dine with him at the palace, including Turkish performers. *Ustad* Munir was among the invitees.

On one occasion, Ataturk and his guests were listening to *Ustad* Munir sing, and Ataturk, sitting in the front row, was so moved by the music that he began to hum along. *Ustad* Munir let him continue for a short while, but when it became apparent that Ataturk had no intention of stopping, *Ustad* Munir signaled the musicians to stop.

Turning to the president, he quietly addressed Ataturk. "Mr. President, only one of us can sing ... and I'm the one on the stage."

The astonished guests were silent. No one could imagine the young singer speaking to the president of the republic in that manner.

Ataturk did not smile. Instead he gave *Ustad* Munir a steely glare and raised his glass of Turkish *rakı*, the anise-flavored distillate so loved in Turkey still today, in a silent sign of acquiescence. But it was clear to all that he was not pleased by the unmistakable request.

Ustad Munir once again signaled to the musicians to play, picking up where they had stopped, and completed his performance. When it was over, Ataturk said good night to his guests but pointedly ignored *Ustad* Munir. Everyone left wondering what would happen.

Some months passed without *Ustad* Munir being invited to return to the palace. But fate would bring these two back together one more time.

In the provincial capital of Bursa, in western Turkey, a grand new hotel had been built to respond to the needs of businessmen, now in favor with the Turkish government which was trying to build up the economy and encourage economic self-sufficiency. There was to be a grand opening of the hotel, with honored guests and dignitaries in attendance for an evening of dining and deal-making. *Ustad* Munir was, of course, the star performing artist, and attended the glittering reception prior to his concert. As he and the other guests mingled, the president's motorcade pulled up, and Ataturk himself came in the door with his aides and security guards. He spotted *Ustad* Munir immediately and nodded in greeting, but the two didn't exchange words.

Many in the crowd already knew of the exchange at the presidential palace in Ankara and waited nervously to see what would happen. They didn't have long to wonder.

Raising his voice Ataturk spoke. "*Ustad* Munir! Good evening, good evening. Would you come over here for a moment?"

Dressed in his usual formal performance clothes, *Ustad* Munir silently walked over to the president and stopped in front of him.

Signaling a waiter, Ataturk took a glass of *rakı* from the tray of drinks and handed it to the singer. "Now, *Ustad* Munir, would you return to the corner across the room from where you came?"

Doing as he was asked, *Ustad* Munir strode back to the other side of the room. The crowd was silent.

"Now, *Ustad* Munir," Ataturk said politely. "Please take the glass of *rakı* and put it on top of your head."

Ustad Munir complied.

With that, Ataturk took a sip of his own *rakı*, reached into his inner coat pocket and pulled out a long-barreled pistol. Slowly raising it up, he aimed it at *Ustad* Munir's glass of *rakı*. Everyone froze.

Slowly Ataturk cocked the pistol and brought the barrel down until it pointed directly at the singer's head with the glass of *rakı* resting on top. The other guests watched silently, frozen in terror.

Taking careful aim, Ataturk slowly began to squeeze the trigger, and just before the shell exploded from the chamber, he raised the pistol and fired over the glass.

Ustad Munir didn't flinch. Instead, he slowly reached up and took the glass off his head and walked slowly toward Ataturk. Standing in front of the founder of modern Turkey, he said, "Mr. President, if you had shot me, you would be known only as the man who killed the finest singer in Turkey." And the two men raised their glasses and drank.

The story always ends there. Whether anything else was said, whether the performance took place, whether the two men shook hands—nothing. Occasionally, when I heard the story in the 1980s told by someone new, they would assure me that they had been to the now old hotel in Bursa and had seen a bullet hole in one wall, covered by a painting. So the story is still told in Turkey, and that's how great stories and great men become larger than life.

BANGLADESH

CHAPTER 17

Ready, Aim … Recite!

When I arrived in 1985 as public affairs officer in Dhaka, Bangladesh, I had hardly unpacked my luggage when I got a call from my Bangladeshi secretary, Farida, telling me that some group wanted me to be the 'chief guest' at their function that same day.

"Farida, I just got off a plane after sitting in a little box for twenty hours. I'm tired and not too coherent. What is this group and what does being 'chief guest' involve?"

"Oh, it's a very prestigious group, sir, composed of intellectuals who hold monthly meetings, and they've called me for the third time since they heard that a new PAO was coming. And as for being chief guest, it's no big deal. You'll get served the little appetizers first, and the president will welcome you, and you can make some polite remarks about being there even though you just got off the plane—it shouldn't take more than an hour."

"I don't know, Farida. I usually like to know more about the groups that invite me, and I always involve my staff in suggesting the kind of remarks that are expected."

"Oh, I don't think that's necessary, sir. This is a very nice group of men, and many of them are well-traveled. And, well, I promised you'd be there. They were so persistent!"

Even a blind man can read the writing on the wall. "Okay. How long before a car picks me up?"

"Well, sir, your plane was on time, so you can lie down and rest for half an hour. I've already told your cook—you've met him?—to have tea ready for you."

Yes, I had met him, or at least I thought I did. "There were three men in white uniforms, but I'm not sure which one was the cook."

"His name is Barua, and I'll call and tell him to come reintroduce himself and to have the tea ready in half an hour. The houseboy will bring it up to you. His name is Lawrence. And you met the outside servant, Christopher. Lawrence and Christopher are Christians, and Barua is a Buddhist."

I'd obviously misjudged the pace of my social life before I had come. My Bengali lessons had been abbreviated; foreign service officers going to Bangladesh were given only courtesy-level language training, since so many Bangladeshis spoke English.

But I'd also missed learning the cultural cues that come with spending time with a native speaker. So I felt a little uneasy about having to perform with so little preparation. I lay down on the queen-sized bed, curtained off with fine-mesh cotton to prevent mosquitoes from feasting on me, and I was out like a light.

"*Sahib*, are you awake?" filtered through the fog of sleep. There was a young man holding a tray with hot tea and cookies.

"Lawrence?"

"Yes, *sahib*. The car is on the way. Farida *memsahib* said to bring you tea."

"Thanks, Lawrence. Just put it on the table here. I'm going to jump into the shower quickly. Can you open my bags and find some clean underwear and a shirt—oh, and a matching tie? You'll find a sport coat in the bag. Just hang it up, and it will relax its own wrinkles." I'd forgotten to ask Farida about what to wear but decided to err on the more dressy side for a group of well-traveled intellectuals. But I learned: no one else would be so stupid as to wear a coat and tie in the usually hot, humid climate. This would be the last time I wore them in Bangladesh in anything except the dead of a 40-degree "winter."

"I'll be downstairs in fifteen minutes."

"Yes, *sahib*."

I made it: clean shirt, tie, coat, and, I think, matching socks.

I already felt odd; I wasn't used to having servants appear noiselessly in my bedroom or go through my suitcase, but that was obviously my problem not his.

The car was parked in my carport. Delwar, the driver, had quietly backed it in so as soon as I was in the car he could exit the driveway without accidentally hitting a rickshaw or donkey cart on the street outside my house. I would later learn that Delwar was an accomplished, conscientious driver, a quiet professional who was used to safely delivering demanding and overly time-conscious Americans to their destinations.

We pulled up at the appointed place just fashionably late.

As I approached the door, it dawned on me that I had forgotten to ask Farida the name of the person I was to meet. No need: a welcoming committee was just inside the door and, with smiles all around, introduced themselves. They professed great pleasure at being the first to welcome me to Bangladesh, asked about my trip, the time I'd spent in travel, etc. Nothing I couldn't handle, thank God ...

Trays of *pakoras*, potato-filled fried dough with chutney dip, appeared as well as glasses of orange soda. This was a Muslim country, after all, especially in public. Promptly at the prescribed hour, the president took me by the arm, and we walked to a speaker's podium. After the requisite warm words of welcome, he proudly said, "And now Mr. Grimland will tell us what he thinks."

"About what?" I muttered inwardly. I started with the usual thanks, my honor at being invited, and my hope to learn more about the organization, etc., etc., etc. I managed to stretch that to six or seven minutes, and then came to the end of my last impromptu sentence.

Silence.

"Oh, Lord, deliver me," I pleaded inwardly.

Silence.

"Uh ... I'm told that you gentlemen are a group of intellectuals. I have never managed to attain that exalted status, so I would like to ask you gentlemen a favor."

Did I sense a mild interest?

"I know that Rabindranath Tagore is your Nobel Prize-winning national poet. My Bengali is not good enough to understand any of his poems in the language in which he wrote them, but if any of you could educate me by quoting part or one of his poems, I would be the wiser for it." I'd had only a quick introduction to Tagore's works in language training, so I was truthfully admitting my ignorance. Not only might I learn something, but it would give them the spotlight.

The president smiled and deferred to another of the members. "Mr. Chowdhury is learned in the great Tagore's works," he said. "Perhaps he would honor us with a brief recitation for your sake."

Mr. Chowdhury was prepared and came to the podium.

"In honor of our distinguished chief guest's arrival in our country, I am glad to be asked to recite a few of Tagore's relevant lines in English."

I thanked him and waited.

"And when I've finished, perhaps Mr. Grimland will honor us with a recitation of one of his favorite American poets?"

I choked. I hadn't memorized poetry since I was in high school, and our English teacher made us memorize and recite numerous lines from Shakespeare's plays—and then only under duress. Besides, Shakespeare wasn't American. My mind frantically cast around until it came to rest on the obvious: as a junior in high school, I had been moved by the African American poet of the 1920s, James Weldon Johnson, and had memorized one of his poems, "The Creation." This poem was included in Johnson's collection, *God's Trombones: Seven Negro Sermons in Verse.* Even though I had loved that poem in particular, and even occasionally recited it, it was hardly the freshest thing in my mind at the moment.

So while Mr. Chowdhury recited Tagore, I worked at mentally resurrecting the lines, hoping that an African American preacher's sermon would fit in this Muslim culture.

Mr. Chowdhury finished, applause was duly offered, and the room went silent for me.

Well, I thought, this may be a short tour if this isn't appropriate, and I'm arrested for proselytizing because I recited a Christian poem. But I was in too deep now to back out. Summoning up all the resonance I could, I launched into "The Creation."

> And God stepped out on space
> He looked around, and he said:
> I'm lonely—I'll make me a world ...

The poem is not long, perhaps four minutes, but it is beautifully crafted. I am not sure to this day whether I got it right, but James Weldon Johnson was not likely to be well-known in Bangladesh, so all I had to do was get the main body of the text and work to keep the syllables that gave it that beautifully poetic rhythm. The men in the room listened intently, and the "Amen" had obviously confirmed that I'd finished. But there were a few moments of silence—I like to think it was thoughtful silence—and then they gave me an enthusiastic round of applause. As for me, I was gratified that

I'd made it through the poem without giving away my possible lapses in memory. My heretofore clean shirt, however, would not lie; it was now stained with patches of sweat, fortunately hidden by the unnecessary coat.

The next day I went to the office. Word of my success had preceded me, and the welcomes from my new staff were warm, hearty—and relieved. The new boss had not embarrassed them; in fact, he'd become somewhat of a minor celebrity. The draft press release about my arrival and position as public affairs officer now contained a small story about my singular success on my first day in the community, including a complimentary quote from the organization's president about my erudition.

I suggested that we all crowd into the press section, our largest room, where I could talk with them. My remarks went something like this:

"I thank you for arranging a successful initiation yesterday, but in future I would prefer knowing more about what is expected of me in the way of speaking. I was lucky yesterday, but I would hate to depend on luck rescuing me every time."

They solemnly promised to do as I'd asked. But once I had achieved renown as a public speaker, my staff was not always able to accommodate my desire to be briefed and given time to prepare something meaningful. Slowly I came to realize that this was exactly the point: in Bangladeshi culture—he who can intelligently extemporize is more highly regarded than he who comes with a canned speech. And you can seldom go wrong in reciting a poem that fits the occasion. That, however, requires having a mental sack full of poems from which to choose and using them appropriately! Bangladesh is a poor country in economic terms, but it is rich in an oral tradition that Americans have long neglected.

So I began to spend some homework time boning up on short American poems or parts of poems from Whitman to Ferlinghetti. I photocopied the longer ones, and occasionally used them as cheat-sheets, but I almost always had the feeling that I'd passed muster.

What greater compliment can you pay to a culture that is ready to speak intelligently at will than to mimic it? Of course Bangladeshi politicians are no different than any others; they can be just as filled with bombast and vanity as anyone. But a quick wit and tongue would seldom be taken amiss.

Amen, amen ...

CHAPTER 18

The Kindness of Strangers

Until I arrived in Bangladesh, I'd never flown to, from, or within any countries in the South Asian subcontinent and therefore had no idea of the adventures that could ensue. In some ways, flying Bangladesh's national carrier, Biman Airlines, was a mild reminder of one's mortality; every time the plane took off, the pilot would come on to greet the passengers, state the duration of the flight, weather conditions, and the scheduled arrival time at the destination, ending with the traditional Arabic expression *Inshallah* ("God willing"). It was considered improper to state a certainty, in this case the timing of our anticipated arrival, when indeed it was a certainty only if God willed it. Westerners sometimes found this unsettling, as it made arrival at our destination seem less certain.

The truth of this uncertainty was apparent on one of my last flights on Biman. Ironically, I contributed to the problem.

As I was finishing my three-year assignment in Bangladesh, I learned that my next post had already been decided: I was to move from being the overall director, public affairs officer of our small USIS post in Dhaka, to becoming the deputy public affairs officer in New Delhi, India, Bangladesh's next-door neighbor and the largest USIS post in the world. I don't remember the exact numbers, but it was something like a dozen

American officers in New Delhi and three other cities, plus six hundred or so Indian employees from graphic arts specialists to librarians, secretaries, and administrative support, and twenty or so drivers. Our entire American and Bangladeshi staff in Dhaka, three American staffers and about fifteen Bangladeshis, would not have taken up more room than the large New Delhi library.

Given the much larger program and management duties, I wanted to go to India and spend a few days getting to know the new challenges I would face. So I made arrangements to visit.

On my travel day I met our travel specialist and expediter, Mr. Sharif, at the airport and gave him my passport to negotiate the sometimes hectic procedures of checking in at the airlines counter and getting my papers through Bangladeshi immigration and customs. As anyone who has traveled overseas knows, local immigration and customs officials could be overly rule-bound about processing travelers in hopes of getting a tip to grease the experience.

No sooner had I turned over my passport than I saw several Bangladeshis whom I knew waiting for the same flight, so I went over to visit with them while waiting for Mr. Sharif to take care of business. He apologized that it would take a few moments longer since he had another embassy employee for whom he had to do the same thing. The other American was traveling to Nepal on a different plane, leaving about the same time as mine, and he hadn't yet arrived at the airport. Since the Bangladeshi guards had seen me arrive in an embassy car, they kindly waved me and my Bangladeshi traveling companions into the VIP departure lounge, where we continued talking.

We were deep in conversation during the first boarding announcement. Fortunately Mr. Sharif, looking a little harried, turned up and handed me my passport and boarding card. Continuing my conversation, I simply slipped them in my suit coat pocket and wandered toward the door leading to the tarmac where our plane awaited. As we reached the roll-on steps to the plane, I pulled my boarding card from my coat pocket, glancing at it to note my seat number. Still conversing with one of the Bangladeshis, I again failed to check my passport, which I could feel in my coat pocket—a careless error—but I was confident in Mr. Sharif's efficiency.

The flight crew gave us the usual safety talk while the engines started their warm-up. Finally obeying that nagging inner voice, I pulled my passport from my pocket as the plane began to roll toward the takeoff spot. The noise of the engines signaled that we were speeding up for a takeoff. Staring at my passport, I realized with shock that the photo staring back at me was an African American.

My mind whirled trying to digest this undeniable difference when I suddenly remembered that I had heard one of the embassy's communication staffers, a black American, telling someone that he was flying to Kathmandu for a temporary duty assignment. Obviously this was that guy staring back at me in the photograph.

Unbuckling my seat belt I jumped up and ran to the cockpit door. This was before the days when I would have been tackled by someone thinking I was hijacking the plane. Knocking on the cockpit door just as the plane stopped prior to taking off, I opened it to see two startled pilots going through their pre-takeoff instrument checks.

"Look!" I shouted over the increasing noise of the engines, "I've got the wrong passport!" Adding unnecessarily, "This guy is black! That's not me! Please: turn the aircraft around and go back to the terminal. I won't be able to get into India with this passport!"

"Please, Sahib," the captain replied. "We are too far into our takeoff procedure to return you to the terminal, and it is against all rules for us to let you off the plane out here on the runway. Please, Sahib. It's no problem. We will radio ahead to New Delhi and explain. They will send someone from your embassy, and they will see to it that everything is done correctly, and you will be allowed in. No problem, sir. Please return to your seat immediately."

Grumbling to myself, I stalked back to my seat and buckled myself in. I was on the verge of wanting to jump out and beat our travel arranger on the head with the first piece of bamboo cane I could find, but as I calmed down I had to admit that I should have checked my travel documents when he gave them back to me. This same scene was probably being played out on an airplane carrying the other guy to Nepal, as he looked at his papers and realized he was holding the wrong passport.

The flight to New Delhi was about two hours, plenty of time for the promised radio call to be relayed to our embassy weekend duty officer. I could imagine him getting a phone call from the Delhi tower saying they had this white man on board carrying a black man's passport, and would they please send someone down to bail him out.

We landed without incident, and one of the flight crew took me to the terminal, only to find out that there were no customs personnel on duty—evidently a slow travel day. "Well, sir, you can call your embassy. There is a pay phone over there."

At that point I realized that I had two problems: first, the pay phone took only special phone tokens, which had to be purchased at a kiosk in the reception hall; and second, I didn't have the embassy phone number with me, only the home number of my promised host. I decided to get a token first.

When I went to the kiosk, there was no attendant. Seeing that the kiosk display panels were open and someone had to be there to see that nothing was taken, I waited. After fifteen minutes or so, the attendant returned and, after some arguing about whether he would accept a $5 bill, the lowest American currency I had, for an Indian phone token worth a few cents, he finally consented.

Grinding my teeth, I flipped through my pocket date book looking for my host's home phone. It was there, but I'd written it hurriedly and had to decipher the poorly scrawled number. Convinced that only prayer would work, I slid my single token into the phone, heard it clink in an empty container box, and waited for a dial tone. Nothing. I hung up, and, fortunately, the phone spat out the token, allowing me to try again. The phone rang and rang and rang—still no answer—and this time no returned token.

Beginning to feel an uncomfortable bit of panic, I went back to the kiosk resigned to paying an exorbitant $5 for another token, but the attendant had obviously returned to his tea break and was nowhere to be seen. There were only half a dozen or so passengers in this huge airport lounge, and I looked around until I saw someone wearing a coat and tie.

"Pardon me, sir, do you speak English? I have a problem."

"Yes, my friend. What can I do to help?" replied the Indian gentleman. I explained my predicament as briefly as I could and asked if by chance he had a phone token.

"Unfortunately, no, I don't, sir," he kindly replied. "But even if I did, you don't know when the gentleman you need to talk to will be at home. Why don't we try to find some senior administrative officer, ask him for the number of the American Embassy, and see if you can make a call on his phone? Come along; I'll help you."

I was so grateful I could have kissed the man's shoes. Undoubtedly, he was one of the beneficent Indian gods charged with taking pity on souls wandering through the Hindu equivalent of purgatory. We indeed found a cooperative senior person who looked up the embassy's phone number and dialed it, handing the phone to me.

The Marine on duty took the call, and after listening to my story, said, "Mr. Grimland, I don't know the man you're trying to reach, but I'll call your USIS duty officer's number and ask him to get someone from the travel office out there as soon as possible. He shouldn't be more than an hour."

It was now midafternoon, but with the help of my new Indian friend, I found a sandwich shop, and he graciously paid for me to get something to eat; I hadn't had anything since breakfast. He had to leave, though, and he promised that when he got home he would call the embassy and make sure all was on track.

It was dark before anyone turned up who could explain to customs officials what had happened and spring me from the reception lounge. The travel expediter's name was Arun, and he had been out with his family on that Sunday afternoon and so had been unreachable until he got home at 6:00 or 7:00 p.m. He had then ordered a car and come to the airport.

Despite the fact that I wasn't black, somehow Arun got me through immigration and customs and even managed to retrieve my single piece of luggage from unclaimed luggage. By the time I got to my host's home, it was 9:30 p.m., and I was a hungry, dirty, and tired traveler. I thanked Arun warmly, knowing we would be working together for the next four years. When I finally went to bed, I said prayers of thanks to all of the Indian gods.

I'd learned lessons that applied not only to traveling in South Asia but to all foreign travel: always carry the phone number of the American embassy; always have a few small American currency bills to barter for necessities; and finally, hope that the culture you're visiting has plenty of specialized gods ready to assist.

CHAPTER 19

Bloodsuckers' Delight

I was working in Bangladesh in 1986, and there not being a lot to do in Dhaka, my friend Bill and I decided to take the short flight up to Nepal to try one of the guided treks in the foothills of the Himalayas. Neither of us had any interest in the hard climbing necessary to get to the Mount Everest base camp, and we definitely did not want the expense of hiring experienced Sherpas.

Bill contacted Pete, his counterpart in Kathmandu, to let him know we were coming and when. Pete knew the country and often entertained visiting colleagues who had much the same goals as we did. He had rented a large house with four or five bedrooms, a garden, and, importantly, a good cook. Pete arranged a nice quiet stroll in mildly elevated country with some great views of peaks in the Himalayas. And we didn't mind a few carriers for our limited gear, as well as a cook and guide. We planned to stay with Pete in Kathmandu prior to heading off on our trek.

Bill and I discussed our plans in the embassy cafeteria and began asking around about equipment we might borrow. Since we weren't looking for real mountaineering gear, it was easy to find what we needed.

Terry, another friend, worked in the embassy's economic assistance program. Three days before we were due to depart, she marched over to our table at lunch and said, "Hey, guys, I hear you're going to Nepal. I'd like to go with you."

"Oh, gee, Terry," Bill and I said pseudo-sadly, "we're already set to go; we've gotten our plane tickets, and, besides, this is a guy thing. We plan to hit the red light district in Kathmandu before heading for the mountains, and we don't think you'll go for that." I made that up on the spot, having no intention of visiting with professional girls, but I hoped that it would dampen her enthusiasm.

"Nope, guys. I'm going. I checked with the airline and booked my ticket on the same flight as you. I'm going with you!"

It flickered through my mind to just say "No, you're not. And if you're on the same damn plane, you're not staying with us in Pete's house." But when it came to confronting a woman like Terry, whose manner had all the finesse of a Mac truck, we were both wusses. Later, we admitted to each other that we should have taken a caveman approach with Terry: "No, woman. Man decides. No girls allowed. Go back and play with your dolls." But I don't think even that would have worked. Terry reserved her diplomatic skills for her job and didn't waste them on taking hints about personal matters.

The day of departure came. We left for the airport, hoping Terry had been bluffing about having a ticket. But no such luck; there she was, sitting at the check-in counter on her backpack, wearing a broad-brimmed hat that made her look like Indiana Jones. I thought I'd say something about this not being a jungle trip, but I was too annoyed to pretend camaraderie, and I learned later that I would have been at least partially wrong.

We landed in Kathmandu, and Pete was waiting for us, looking surprised that there were three of us and that one was a female. But he greeted everyone equally and took us home. Bill and I were assigned to one bedroom, and Terry to her own.

Drinks and dinner loosened the tension some, as did the after-dinner brandy. Whatever we ate was delicious; Nepali cooks are known for their expertise in seasoning. Since we were to leave early the next morning to travel to the starting point of our trek outside of the small western town of Pokhara, Pete suggested we hit the hay earlier than usual. Pete left Bill with a second bottle of good brandy to take on the trip.

The road to Pokhara was like most roads I'd traveled in South Asia: our Hindu taxi driver must have been reincarnated from a former life as a suicide warrior and drove like a bat out of hell, scattering chickens, pigs, and miscellaneous small creatures off the road, occasionally, and reluctantly, giving way to a large bus or truck. It seemed as though we had enough luggage and gear to spend a winter on Everest, and I guess he figured if he hit anything, we could survive a blow better than the other vehicle. He did, however, stop several times for sweet milky tea, the stops being a welcome break from the white-knuckled, bumpy ride.

By the time we reached Pokhara, however, we were ready to relieve ourselves of our loads of tea. For Bill and me, this was no problem; the cleanliness or lack thereof of the restrooms didn't bother us, but Terry was a little more fastidious. She decided she'd wait until we were on the trail.

Our prearranged guide and group of bearers were waiting, anxious to get going since it was early summer, and we were in the lowlands. It would be getting hot soon. So each of the six bearers squatted down on his haunches while his comrades loaded him up with our large backpacks, a supply of clean water, and a small awning, which would provide shade while we ate. The cook carried nothing; he had his own bearer with a small pack of snacks for the trail. By midmorning, we were finally on our way.

Looking ahead, we could see that the track ran down the center of a low valley, gradually sloping up to the first hill about four miles ahead. The valley was flat and narrow, perhaps a hundred yards wide, a carpet of bright green meadow grass bordered with trees on both sides. We could see high mountains in the distance; the highest, Annapurna, was a stunning sight of gray craggy heights, white snowfields, and blue sky overhead.

Bob and I kept commenting on the scenery, trying to be nice and include Terry in the conversation, but she merely grew more and more quiet. After perhaps a mile of this, Terry sidled up to me and whispered, "Dave, I've got to pee—badly!" Since she'd held it back in town, I could understand her problem. "Where can I go?" she said, her voice a little strained. I had to admit she had a problem with privacy but said, "Terry, there's that line of trees fifty yards away. We'll call a halt and rest while you scoot over to the trees and water one." I conveyed this to Bill, and he agreed, so the guide brought the group to a halt and, smiling, gave Terry a small roll of toilet paper. She didn't pause but strode purposefully toward the trees while we sat down in the grass and waited. And waited. And waited.

Suddenly, Terry screamed from the trees. "Oh god. Oh god. Somebody come help me!" This was no ladylike call for minor assistance. The first thing that crossed my mind was that a cobra had bitten her. Bill and I raced for the tree line. (The bearers merely grunted something to each other and grinned as though they knew what had happened.)

As Bill and I reached the trees, Terry stopped screaming, and we couldn't see her. It was like we'd stepped from the meadow into a dark jungle, water dripping off the leaves.

"Terry! Terry! Where are you?"

"Over here," she said in a subdued voice. As we made our way through the undergrowth, she hollered, "No! Don't come here! I don't want you to see me." Bill and I stopped, not knowing what was wrong or what we were supposed to do.

"Terry," Bill shouted. "Are you okay? Where are you? What do you want us to do?"

There was a moment's silence, and then she finally responded. "You guys gotta promise not to laugh. I don't have any pants on. Oh, hell, I guess you've seen a woman's butt before. Just don't make a big thing of it, okay?"

Now I was really puzzled. How had she lost her pants?

As we moved through the wet brush, we finally saw Terry's top half and, sure enough, a pair of pants a little ways away.

"Look, I squatted down to pee and tripped over one of these tree roots," she said. "Then as I got back up I noticed this little worm on my leg, and it won't come off." She gingerly pulled on it to demonstrate. Sure enough it stuck there, wiggling and obviously alive.

Suddenly a light came on in my dim brain. I'd grown up in South Texas, where environments like this were common; they were usually river bottomland, muddy and wet, and occasionally we'd find one of these "worms." As kids we had sometimes been bitten by them but had learned to take a small shaker of salt, dash a little on the critter, and it would almost immediately let go. These were no fishing worms; we used to collect them for students in science classes to dissect. These were leeches.

"Uh, Terry, did you already pee?" I was concerned that if she hadn't, she needed to do so before we began solving the problem.

"Of course," she said. "I was in bad shape. There's the roll of toilet paper over there."

"Terry, those aren't worms, they're blood-sucking leeches. You're going to have to let us look at your rear end and see whether there are more. Whatever you do, don't try to pull them off. They've fastened themselves on to your skin with their teeth, and they excrete an anticoagulant. If you pull off the leech, the wound will not stop bleeding."

Terry literally went white.

"Get up on your knees and let Bill and me examine your backside to see how many you've got. Then we'll go get some salt from the cook and pour it on them. That makes them let go, and we can squash them without leaving you with their teeth and an oozing blood spot."

Terry did as she was told, too afraid to curse. There must have been fifty leeches on her buttocks, all hungrily sucking away.

"Uh, Terry, we've got a problem here. Bill, run get some salt—lots of it—and get back as soon as you can. Terry, just stay kneeling and still. The leeches drop out of the wet leaves on the trees and fasten on to anything that's skin. Here, I'll pull your pants over right beside you, and you get as much of your legs in the pants as you can."

Bill disappeared. I could imagine him trying to explain to the guide and cook that he needed lots of salt. But I remembered the grins of the bearers as Terry left, and I figured there wouldn't be much explaining necessary.

Bill reappeared with a generous sack of salt, Terry leaned over into his arms while I whittled the end of a small stick flat enough to scoop out the salt, and then applied the salt to the leeches. They immediately let go, and I was able to squash them between my fingertips before they switched victims.

"How many are there?" Terry whimpered.

"Enough. You don't really want to know. Stay still; the salt will fall off if you move."

"Are they just on my butt?"

"I think so, but when we finish removing what we can see, you're going to have to examine yourself for any that might have crawled inside. I assume you don't feel anything wiggling, do you?" While a good screenwriter could have made a humorous scene out of this, I was concerned because neither my high school biology course nor my limited personal experience with leeches had gone into more detail about just whether or how far leeches could crawl into a body cavity. Nor did I have any idea whether there were dangerous bacteria on the leeches or their rings of tiny teeth. I didn't want to deal with the possibility of infection in one of Terry's intimate openings. So I said nothing and hoped for the best. If she started to show signs of an infection, we had some antibiotics and could start her on those while we worked our way down to a doctor.

"But what about you guys?" Terry said. "If they fall out of the trees, you might have some on you, too."

"I don't think so, Terry. Both Bill and I have been wearing lightweight long-sleeved shirts, and leeches look for skin. But we'll take our shirts off when get out of the trees and shake them out, as well as look each other over."

What was nice in this exchange was that Terry forgot for a moment her own troubles and thoughtfully considered what problems we might have.

The shaking out and mutual exams proved us clear of leeches, and so we rejoined the group of bearers, shouldered our light packs, and moved on. I noticed that Terry took a fast-paced lead. She obviously wanted to be out of the lowlands before she had to relieve herself again, and I couldn't blame her.

We reached the base of the steeper slope without incident and got up into the higher elevations before stopping for lunch. I thought I felt a wriggling here or there, but, fortunately, it was all in my head. We were out of trouble now.

The rest of the four-day trek proved uneventful. Terry showed no signs of an infection and gulped down slightly more than her share of our one bottle of brandy. We dined on fish-tasting eggs: the Nepalese feed fish meal to their chickens, giving them a distinctive taste. We saw only a few other trekkers and were alone with the gorgeous scenery. By the time we descended back to the lowlands and got a taxi for the return to Kathmandu, we were much better acquainted than we had been. All it took was a few leeches between friends.

CHAPTER 20

Father Charlie: A Pennsylvania Irishman in Rural Bangladesh

I met a Catholic priest and missionary in our embassy lunchroom in Dhaka, Bangladesh. The lunchroom was a little more crowded than usual, but he was sitting alone at one of the tables eating an American hot dog and drinking a Coke, so I asked if he minded if I joined him. "Of course not," he replied with a twinkle in his eye. "I love hot dogs, and they're not available in Bangladesh."

I'd been in Dhaka about a year but had not seen the priest before. I got my customary soup and rice, and we visited while we ate. It turned out that Father Charlie was a White Father, assigned to oversee the Catholic Church and the elementary education program in a small village not far from Dhaka. Not knowing what a "White Father" was, I did the natural thing and asked him. I'd learned the hard way not to pretend to know something I didn't.

Father Charlie explained that the White Fathers is an order of missionary priests founded in 1868 by Roman Catholic Cardinal Charles Lavigerie to proselytize in northern Africa.

Following the customary dress of the native inhabitants of North Africa, they wore distinctive white robes to stay a little cooler in hot climates.

Father Charlie was an American with a large dollop of Irish ancestry from a small Pennsylvania town who had been assigned to Bangladesh some dozen years before. He ministered to the Bangladeshis in a village accessible during the monsoon season only by small boat. He didn't think there was a road to the village even in the dry season, since rivers were a more practical mode of travel. Whenever he came into Dhaka—a day's boat ride—he made sure to leave time to come by for his hot dog with old baseball park style French's mustard. Second on his list of pleasures was a double serving of vanilla ice cream, which, like his hot dog and Coke, was also not then available in Bangladesh.

Over several weeks, Father Charlie showed up at the embassy several times, the ambassador evidently having given him permission to avail himself of the embassy lunchroom. Few restaurants in Dhaka catered to foreigners except the two five-star hotels. These hotels would likely be beyond his means and wouldn't have hot dogs anyway.

I made polite conversation, but not being Catholic, made no attempt to push myself on him. I was interested in village life, since my job was entirely centered in Dhaka, where the press and universities were situated. Not being in the aid business I seldom got out into the countryside, which I admitted. Finally, he asked me, "Would you like to come out to my village and see the real Bangladesh?" He seemed a gentle, likable man, and I took his invitation to be a sincere one.

I decided it was too good a chance to miss. "Sure," I said. "When is it convenient for you? I wouldn't want to show up on a day you are planning on coming to Dhaka and cause you to miss out on your hot dog. Would you mind if I brought along

Jess, one of my American trainees? He knows no more about rural Bangladesh than I do."

He laughed. "Of course I wouldn't mind if Jess joins you. I have lots of room in the church guest quarters. And good company is always better than hot dogs and ice cream! So tell me when you'll be able to get away from the affairs of state here in the big city, and I'll plan to be there." I suggested a date for a two-day visit, and we were on.

He told me to have my driver bring us to a boat departure/landing point. It would be a four- or five-hour trip, depending on the weather, so the driver should find us a typical country boat with a tightly woven split cane cover to protect us from sun or rain.

"What can I bring?" I asked. "Oh, don't worry," Father Charlie replied. "But if you feel it socially necessary, you could bring a good bottle of whiskey. It's good medicine for whatever ails you."

I was a little surprised. Growing up in south Texas, I'd not been around Irish American Catholic priests; our small town Presbyterian minister would not likely have asked for a bottle of bourbon as a house gift. But what the heck. If I had been living in a Bangladeshi village, I might have asked for a case of anything alcoholic. And while I'd learned to like Bangladeshi food as prepared by my cook, every time I tried it as a guest in a Bangladeshi home, my gut would object for the next day or two to the hot peppers and mustard oil used in preparing it. Taking something "medicinal" along on this trip might prove wise.

So Charlie and I shook hands; he had already suggested I drop the "Father" honorific. "It's too hot to speak formally," he chuckled, and I promised to make the boat at the appointed day.

It was a beautiful winter day, meaning it was not broiling hot and humid. We'd brought bottles of water and sandwiches for the journey and were glad we had. Gliding along the river, we were surrounded by the beautiful Bangladesh scenery with both greenery and flowers. *Shimul, or* "cotton silk," trees with flame-red flowers and bare branches were visible from the boat along the riverbanks when there was nothing to obscure them. We pulled up at the village's landing at midafternoon; several little boys scurried away to inform the father that his visitors had arrived. They grabbed our overnight packs, scuffling over who would get the honor of carrying what. Mine was the heavier, with two whiskey bottles—Jess and I had decided that since there were two of us, we ought to double the house gift— and our heavy packs evidently meant to the boys that we must be important guests.

It was a short walk to the surprisingly impressive church, where Charlie emerged from a large shaded porch and greeted us with a big grin. Guessing at what our packs carried, he warned the boys not to horse around with them, and then said, "Let me show you your room, and then we'll come back to the porch and have some lemonade."

The room, one of perhaps half a dozen, was indeed spacious, with twin beds covered by thin-meshed mosquito nets. A washstand was fed by water from the village well. Charlie assured us it was as pure as a Pennsylvania mountain stream. I was a little nervous about that assertion, but what was I to do? I'd be drinking lemonade in a few minutes, and dinner would follow, with further need for something to drink. Well, I thought, what's a little diarrhea among friends? Maybe water that's as pure as the water that comes from a Pennsylvania mountain stream and is consumed in a church as well would kill any Bangladeshi parasites. Besides, everything I saw, including the bathrooms, one to every four or five rooms, had been spotlessly cleaned for us honored guests.

We returned to the porch, where we passed around lemonade with little sweet cookies, and talked about the trip. Since it was winter, the shadows started deepening early; women came out to light the lanterns as well as put a match to mosquito coils.

Once lit, the flame would go out, and the coil would slowly smolder, the smoke hardly visible but containing a pesticide that kept mosquitoes at more than arm's length. I had these in my home in Dhaka—everyone did. There are healthier things to breathe than pesticide smoke, but taking a chance on getting malaria didn't hold much appeal either.

As the land turned dark, I was surprised that it also turned much cooler than I expected, evidently because we were away from the city structures that radiated back the day's heat. Everyone brought out a light shawl, and Jess and I returned to the room to dig out sweaters and decided to bring back the whiskey to the porch. Fresh glasses were delivered, and, while a group of church ladies brought out steaming bowls of rice and curried lamb, Charlie poured a generous dollop of scotch into our glasses. Following his example we sipped our drinks, the alcohol pleasantly warming us against the night chill.

"So, Charlie," I said. "What's our program for tomorrow?"

"Well, I thought I'd take you round and show you the church first, and then we'll visit the classrooms. The children know you're coming, of course, and are anxious to put on a program for you."

Even though I'd only been in Bangladesh a year, I knew of this custom. On the day after my arrival, a Washington visitor from the Voice of America's Bangla language broadcast division had come to Dhaka, and we had taken him out to a nearby village for the dedication of a small stone monument inscribed in English and Bangla with the visitor's name, date, and an emphatic assertion that he had indeed been there. He had come because Bangladesh had more VOA Listening Clubs than any country in the world, radio being the chief form of rural entertainment at that time. The VOA official had brought boxes of VOA pens and notepads, and a few baseball caps for the club's officers. After the presentation of gifts, the club members did a little program of welcoming music and traditional dancing. So I anticipated a similar welcome from the school kids.

Jess and I were indeed hungry, having had only sandwiches all day, so we dug into the rice and curry, literally, with our fingers. I knew of this manner of eating, having seen Bangladeshi guests at dinners in my home, but I usually provided myself and anyone else who preferred with a fork or spoon.

But out here we followed Charlie's example: we rolled the rice into little balls with our fingers and then scooped up a few vegetables and pieces of lamb and stuffed the dripping rice ball awkwardly into our mouths. Eating with one's fingers is relatively easy with fried chicken or hamburgers, but getting a semi-soupy mixture of rice and curry from plate to mouth was trickier. We managed it with only a minor drip or two on our sweaters. Charlie, well-practiced, didn't spill a drop on his white robe.

Grateful for the food, which fortunately had not been too peppery, we finished dinner with some syrup-covered sweets and a few more sips of whiskey. It was now completely dark, and rather than waste lamp kerosene, we agreed that bed was the proper destination. Jess and I were indeed tired. You wouldn't expect a boat ride and short walk around the grounds to give us much excuse, but we were ready for bed. We made our way to our room with flashlights, and before the mosquito nets had stopped fluttering, we were asleep.

Charlie met us at the porch the next morning, and we had breakfast. A couple of hard-boiled eggs, papayas, and hot sugared tea with milk set us up for the day.

The school day had already started; it was obvious that the kids were expecting us. I'm guessing there were about twenty classrooms of seven- to nine-year-olds, a man or woman teacher for each class, and wooden desks or long tables made by village carpenters. Each classroom featured old-fashioned chalk blackboards; they really weren't much different from the schools I'd gone to in south Texas. The children's behavior was impeccable. They all stood up as Charlie, Jess, and I entered the room, where we were led to chairs at the front and introduced to the teacher. The whole room of children then recited a greeting in English and Bangla.

In these rural schools, no homework assignments were handed in. Paper, even for schoolwork, was expensive and limited. Instead the kids stood and recited their answers to the math or history or language questions. The teachers spoke English, and the children responded in kind, although when something particularly important was said, the teacher usually switched to Bangla.

Repeating this as we made our way to all the classrooms took up most of the morning. Just before the noon break, we were ushered into the school yard, and various groups of kids— the young girls dressed in their best with fresh flowers in their hair—stepped out in front of their classmates and performed a little song or dance or made more formal speeches of welcome in English.

I was surprised by how much English the children knew, but I remembered that Bangladesh had been colonized by the British, and British missionaries had designed the educational system. Confident that the King's English was superior to any local dialect in the countries they ruled, they had insisted that the natives learn English. In fact, the Bangladeshi youngster or adult who knew English had a far better chance of success than someone who knew only Bangla.

The national poet of both Bangladesh and East Bengal in India, Rabindranath Tagore, had received the Nobel Prize for Literature in 1918. He had written his poetry in Bangla and English, but when his work was recited by Bangladeshis, it was more a matter of education that determined in which language the recitation would take place. Bangladeshi intellectuals could recite Tagore's poetry in either Bangla or English and seldom missed a chance to demonstrate their pride in having been home to this distinguished man.

Following the youngsters' performances, they took their noon break, everyone sitting on the ground and unwrapping a clean cloth with fruit and what I assumed was a rice flour cake or bread.

As the kids finished their lunches, a crowd of villagers appeared in the open area around the church, next to where we were sitting. I asked Charlie whether they had come for some special Mass—it wasn't Sunday—but more and more people were arriving, obviously focused on the church. Charlie replied, "No, we're not celebrating Mass. They've come to see you and Jess. We don't get that many visitors out here; word has gotten around that they'll be able to see and perhaps greet you."

Sure enough, people started coming up and greeting us, and because Jess and I had each had a couple of months of Bangla language training in Washington, we were, to their delight, able to reply in simple Bangla. The crowd kept growing, and someone brought out a small band of drums and a marimba, with a couple of singers accompanied by a small harmonium.

All together, I would guess there were between five hundred and one thousand people milling about. "Father Charlie!" I exclaimed. "Where have all these people come from? You told us the village you served was small!"

He laughed. "I told you people would be curious," he said. "These people are from other villages, some several miles away. Today is likely to go down in local myth as 'The Day the Visitors Came.'"

By the time the socializing had finished, the evening shadows lengthened, and people started leaving. A few seemed to have come too far to walk home that evening, so impromptu homemade tents and little cooking fires began to appear.

"Come on, Dave," Charlie warned. "We'd better get back to the porch, or you'll be invited to stay and share their pretty meager traveling supper. I think we can do a little better back near the church."

Waving and shaking hands and smiling our good-byes, we made our way back to our more private area, where we were served a different curry and rice and, of course, a little more of the whiskey to warm us up.

In the little I'd been outside of Dhaka, I had seen how quickly small clusters of people could appear if we stopped to rest on the roads. They were not threatening, just curious, wanting to watch us eat or water a local tree (we drew the line there). After all, Bangladesh had a population then of about one hundred million people in a country just a little smaller than the state of Illinois, with a population density of twenty-seven hundred people per square mile compared to Illinois's five hundred.

Again, Jess and I went to bed impressed but exhausted by all the hand-shaking and being the objects of attention for the larger part of the afternoon.

The next day was Sunday. We had planned to depart after attending the church service with Father Charlie presiding. The huge edifice was packed, partially by people who had camped overnight and partly by folk from nearby. We had a light lunch, packed our things, and warmly invited Charlie to the embassy lunchroom the next time he drifted down river, promising to have an extra bottle of whiskey for him to bring back home.

The trip back to the Dhaka landing was uneventful, but when Jess and I got to the office a few days later, we raided our supplies for a couple of boxes of ruled legal pads and as many boxes of pencils as we could cram into a shipping box for the school kids. Our library even brought over a few basic books about the United States, with maps and pictures the village teachers could use with their lessons.

It had been another serendipitous learning experience I was coming to expect with foreign service life. Most of the people we had met were poor beyond anything we had ever seen, but they were hospitable, and, just as importantly, they were proud of their country and its heritage. They had dignity, and they'd shared what they had with us. On a subsequent visit to Dhaka, we asked Charlie what happened when the children finished their middle schooling years in villages like his, which had a church school.

"Most of them will return home to help their parents work the land," he said. "A few will be sent to relatives in a larger town and continue through high school, and a tiny minority will come to Dhaka to go to the university on a state-paid scholarship. The money you pay your servants is probably sent back to their villages and saved for educating the younger siblings. But it's a difficult life: many of them will get into drugs or bad company, they'll learn to like drinking, and jobs will be scarce for them. The average life expectancy is around age forty-five, and the population keeps growing. Americans just don't know how good we have it."

No, Charlie, we don't.

INDIA

CHAPTER 21

Sleeping with a Sikh in Calcutta

My first real acquaintance with Sikhs was not long after I had been posted to New Delhi. Our landlord was an older Sikh, but we had only an introductory cup of tea; I didn't have any further acquaintance with him.

The first time I engaged with a Sikh more closely was when I had to fly from Dehli to Calcutta. Indians were always going on strike for some reason or another; the day before I was due to leave for Calcutta, the newspapers reported that the next day there would be a general strike of all transportation workers. We'd heard many such strikes announced and then at the last minute get called off, so I decided to go to the airport for my afternoon flight and keep my fingers crossed that it would leave.

Indeed it did leave, and so I settled down for the two-hour flight and began to snooze. I was awakened by the captain's voice on the intercom: "Ladies and gentlemen, we have just received word that the transportation strike will begin in fifteen minutes."

He paused, and some of us wondered if they would continue to fly the plane or, less drastically, choose an alternate airport halfway to Calcutta and land there.

To our relief, the captain came back on and announced, "We have conferred and decided that since it's only another hour, we will continue to Dum Dum airport in Calcutta and land."

The captain continued. "Although we are told that control tower personnel will guide us to a safe landing, we are not likely to have baggage crews to unload the aircraft. You will have to get your own luggage and carry it to the terminal." That didn't sound too bad; it certainly beat landing in some offbeat place with no hotel or overnight facilities.

We touched down a little late, just as darkness was closing in. Because the captain obviously did not want to bring the plane back to the terminal, where it might be attacked by angry strikers who spotted a plane landing after the strike had been called, he took the plane to the end of the runway before killing the engines. At that point, the entire flight crew, including the captain and copilot, came through the cabin and opened the doors to let everyone out, but they were the first to leave! After all, they had nothing but their flight bags to retrieve and carry. They disappeared into the growing darkness.

The rest of us deplaned, and looked with some disbelief at the distance we had to walk—at least a mile back to the terminal. Fortunately, one of the passengers knew how to get into the luggage hold, so after getting the door open, several of us clambered up and passed down luggage to the other passengers. There were very few rolling bags back in the late 1980s, so men, women, and children all lugged a bag or box they'd checked, and off we slow-marched the half hour walk back to the terminal.

As we entered the terminal building, we were discouraged to find the main waiting room crowded with people, some of whom like us had landed and walked from their plane, and others who had come to the airport to depart on a flight, found that it wouldn't leave, and were stuck when they couldn't get a taxi or a bus back to the city after the strike was called.

It was a chaos of crying children, with grandmothers sitting on the floor, since there were not enough seats, of course. The toilets were working but looked dangerously overloaded, and there was no one to fix them. If the building had been clean before, it was definitely not so now. Looking around, I decided that I had to try anything to avoid sleeping on the floor of this hot, dirty airport.

I managed to find a phone and called the airport hotel where I had a reservation.

"Oh, yes, sir, Mr. Grimland. We do have a room reserved for you, but we cannot send the hotel car service to get you—the strike, you know. If you can make it here, you may claim your room."

I knew the hotel was another couple of miles down the road toward the city, so with my bag I went out to the curb and studied what might be possible. I did not want to be set upon by *goondas* in the dark. *Goonda* is one of those Hindi words that has wandered into English in a shortened form as "goon."

While I was standing there contemplating my options, a tall turbaned Sikh gentleman in his fifties came out, obviously with a similar problem. He was not in uniform, but he had the bearing of a military officer, and—the dead giveaway—was carrying a swagger stick in the British manner. He was unruffled and walked over to me.

"How do you do, sir? My name is Singh. I think we may have a similar problem." He was speaking perfect upper-class British English.

"I'm afraid we do, sir. I assume you are or were in the Indian army? May I ask your rank to know how to address you?"

"Of course, sir ... I'm now retired Colonel Singh, at your service."

I in turn introduced myself, and his eyes brightened a little at the thought of teaming up with an American diplomat, even though he outranked me. 'Diplomat' often opens unexpected doors.

"I just confirmed, Colonel, that my reserved room at the airport hotel down the road is awaiting my arrival, but they cannot send the hotel car. If you'd like to walk with me, surely the hotel will have another room; with all transportation down, I assume no one could have gotten there."

"Hmmm. Yes, of course ..." He peered into the darkness thoughtfully. "I say, sir, may I call you Mr. Grimland?" I see a couple of luggage carts over there for our bags. Let's put our things in them, lash the carts together with our belts to form a flying wedge, and give it a try. I doubt the unorganized *goondas* will attack two of us, and if they do ..." He slapped his thigh with the swagger stick, pulling the handle end out of the leather padding and exposing a heavy steel eighteen-inch ice pick. "This and our manly resolve will deflect them from their dastardly purpose. By the way, I don't suppose you have a revolver?"

"Uh ... no, Colonel. Diplomats aren't allowed to carry weapons even for self-defense. I wish it were otherwise. But even if we did carry them, it might prove an embarrassment to have to use them."

"Bloody stupid rule, Mr. Grimland, although I'm sure you did not invent it. In India one must always be prepared to take charge of the common classes, and it sometimes requires a little visual encouragement."

With this settled, we set about making our flying wedge of loaded luggage carts weighted down by a couple of bags. Just as we finished tightening our lashing belts, we heard the sound of a vehicle's engine coming out of the darkness toward the terminal. Swinging into the airport drop-off area was an Indian Army jeep—complete with a *jawan* (enlisted soldier) sitting on the back deck of the jeep and manning a mounted .30 caliber machine gun.

The jeep pulled over to where we were standing. Suddenly Colonel Singh smiled broadly and waved at the soldier riding in the front passenger seat of the jeep: "Johnny! What are you doing here?"

After greetings and introductions in staccato Punjabi all around, Colonel Singh explained "This is Johnny Singh, in charge of this patrol. He's the son of one of my comrades in arms. We served together against the Chinese some years ago!"

Now, as a corporal in the Indian Army, Johnny and his two mates were patrolling this road near the Calcutta airport to be sure that strikers didn't shut down the airport completely.

Then to business: "Johnny, would you be a good chap and take us down to the airport hotel? My friend Mr. Grimland is concerned that we might have to break some heads before we got there. I assured him that *goondas* are merely scum, but you know these diplomats." Knowing chuckles all around ...

Johnny and the others, the driver and an additional backseat *jawan,* moved themselves and their army-issue Russian Kalashnikovs over to allow Colonel Singh and me to squeeze in with our luggage, and off we roared. If any *goondas* were lurking in the darkness, they slipped away rather than face a .30 caliber machine gun, three Kalashnikovs, and an ice-pick-wielding retired army colonel.

In less than ten minutes, we pulled up at the hotel. After more good-natured banter, we waved good night to Johnny and his patrol and walked in.

I was wrong about the place not being crowded. The reception area was packed with stranded travelers and their luggage. Wending our way toward the check-in desk, Colonel Singh muttered "Well, I got us here, Mr. Grimland. See whether your diplomatic skills can get us a room. I don't fancy spending the night on one of these public couches."

Reaching into my pants pocket, I extracted an American $20 bill and picked up an Indian magazine from a table. Quickly slipping the bill into the folds of the magazine, I positioned it with just a slip of greenback showing.

Taking the lead, I walked up to the harried check-in clerk, and in a firm but demanding tone announced, "I'm Mr. Grimland from the American Embassy in New Delhi. I spoke to someone at this desk earlier and was assured that my reserved room was ready for check-in if I could get here. If possible, I'd like two rooms, one for myself and one for my Sikh friend here."

The clerk looked stricken. "Oh, sir, I'm so sorry. I had to give all our rooms to some of these tired travelers," waving his arm at the room full of would-be guests.

I slid the magazine over the counter with the green slip of the bill visible to him only. "Nonsense, my good man. Surely you can find just two rooms for a tired diplomat and a hero of the Chinese war?"

"Oh, that I could, sir. But let me check my book again." With furrowed brow, he ran his finger down a sweat-stained ledger.

"I am so sorry, sir. I do find an empty room for you, but there is simply not another for your friend." I glanced over at Colonel Singh, and he nodded.

"All right, then, we'll take it. But the price I agreed to pay was for a private room; I understand there is a discount if two people occupy one room."

The clerk glanced down at the magazine in front of him with its pale green American money just visible and replied, "Well, of course, sir, under these conditions."

"Fine, young man. And we expect some complimentary dinner. We've had nothing to eat."

"Oh, sir. I'll check with the kitchen. This crowd has almost stripped our larders, and we cannot get a delivery truck in with more." He picked up the phone and spoke to the kitchen. "They tell me they have some fine soup left, sir, and some bread baked today. I hope that will suffice. It is, of course, at our expense."

"Fine, sir! You're a most understanding young man. We'll go upstairs and bathe then come down for dinner. No candles are necessary. And please take the magazine; when this confusion is over, I'm sure you'll want something to read and relax with."

"Oh, thank you, sir!" he sputtered, and the magazine disappeared. "We'll have the soup hot, and no candles." He grinned.

The soup was indeed tasty; anything would have been welcome at that time of night. And when Colonel Singh and I got up to leave the dining room, I left an overly generous tip.

We were tired, but sat on our beds in the room and sipped orange soda. Colonel Singh removed his turban. He didn't have to unwrap it; it was sold pre-wrapped and pinned, and he simply slipped it on like a cap. He had long, graying hair tied up in a bun on top of his head, which he now unpinned and brushed out.

He wore a small steel bracelet with a miniature sword dangling from it. Evidently this satisfied the Sikh habit of always carrying a knife.

All the time, we chatted. He had retired from the army and now ran a business making parts for a machine. It was not his inability to explain it in English but rather my total lack of understanding of what the machine was or how it worked. to this day I don't know what his business made. We told each other our life histories and exchanged cards. For several years I received Christmas cards from him and sent him Indian holiday cards, but our contact eventually petered out.

Each of us thanked the other for playing our roles in the evening's little adventure, and as he turned the lights out to go to sleep, he chuckled and said, "It was brilliant of you to think of putting the money in the magazine. But you overpaid, my friend!"

CHAPTER 22

Calcutta

The foreign service did its best to educate me: Istanbul was exotic; Jerusalem was fascinating; Paris beautiful; Athens a living ancient history course; Nicosia presented difficult experiences; London speaks to me in my own language and offers both culture and good food.

But Calcutta is different, like no other city in which I have spent time. It offers a rich history, a Bengali population that numbers many thousands of good English speakers, excellent food, and a vibrant art scene, along with abject poverty and hungry rats.

I was never assigned to Calcutta, but in 1988, when I became the deputy public affairs officer in USIA's largest post in the world, New Delhi, one of my responsibilities was to visit our USIA branch posts in Bombay (now Mumbai), Madras (now Chennai), and Calcutta (now Kolkata). So the memories here involve touching at least the surface of these cities known then by the names given by the British during quarterly visits to each. My visits were usually an occasion for our American officers and their Indian staff to show off the people they knew and the environment in which they worked. The memories here are culled from numerous visits to Calcutta over three years.

And memories there are, including the local PAO who kept a pet mongoose. In some ways it made sense; the mongoose kept the grounds free of snakes. But Becca did not want an outdoor pet and preferred to let the critter run free in the house. Whenever I visited and stayed with her, I could never be sure when sitting down if I'd find a critter hiding in the folds of the couch or under the pillows in my bed.

I'll not repeat the history of Calcutta, since that's readily available online. The commercial, cultural, and educational center of eastern India, it was founded in the seventeenth century by the British East India Company, primarily because of its excellent port. Parts of the city are wealthy, as the tree-lined broad avenues and majestic old homes attest.

But it is also a city of stark contrasts. Driving in from the airport, one passes over what must be the world's largest garbage mountain, constantly smoldering from fires that are occasionally set to control its size. Scores of wooden and plastic shacks sit atop the garbage, each housing a family of ragpickers who have staked out salvage rights to a carefully marked and watched area. They sift through the piles of household waste, animal carcasses, old machinery, broken musical instruments, moldy books, newspapers, and broken toys to see what can be set aside for fixing and resale or taken to recycling centers to be melted down and reincarnated as something usable and new, which in turn will eventually find its way back to the garbage mountain. Children are conceived, born and die on the mountain, but generations of these professional ragpickers make enough to survive and even occasionally prosper. The drive past the mountain from west to east takes about twenty minutes; passengers of any vehicle that has an air conditioner roll up the windows to ward off the smell.

On one of my first trips to our office there, an office car took me on a short morning's tour of the old downtown district. Again it was a study in contrasts: beggars propped plastic sheets against fine masonry walls that hid luxurious homes, and lived there in monsoon or winter weather. Someone always occupied these humble shelters if others in the family were away in order to discourage squatters from claiming the rude shelter as their own.

Most seemed to collect enough coins to buy food to survive, especially if the meager diet was supplemented by trips to neighborhood temples for a daily or weekly meal of the sacrificial animals killed by the priests and cooked into thin stews. Beggars came carrying their own battered tin plates and cups for a pile of stew over rice. These men had no work; they depended entirely on the charity of others.

One of these temples was dedicated to the worship of Kali, the patron goddess of the city. Kali represents death and the consuming aspects of reality. Women in childbirth also pray to her. Kali's fearsome black statue oversaw her temple's courtyard, a scene of semi-chaos. Her preferred sacrifice was said to be the blood of freshly killed goats, so every day, masses of bleating goats waited in a fenced-off enclosure of the temple courtyard, smelling the blood of their recently slaughtered companions and somehow having a premonition of what lay ahead for them. Excrement was everywhere; a frightened goat does what a frightened human would do knowing his death is imminent.

Around the corralled goats, a line of hungry men wove, getting their plates filled with food, dipping their cup in a fountain of water, and squatting on the ground using their right hand to shovel the hot food into empty stomachs. Priests kept track of each man. Second portions were not allowed, and the huge cauldrons could only be filled a limited number of times, so there was an almost palpable sense of resignation from those who didn't get even a single portion.

Other than the pungent smells and bleating goats, my sensory organs picked up nothing from the beggars: no shouting or shoving, no arguments. Some seemed too weak to make much of a fuss about anything. Nor did the priests shout their orders to keep the line flowing. There seemed to be an implicit understanding that making a ruckus was useless.

Ironically, right across the narrow street from Kali's temple was Mother Teresa's Home for the Dying. Mother Teresa's nuns and associates would dicker with rickshaw drivers to take their rickshaws around the city looking for beggars dying on the streets. The rickshaw-*wallah*, "*wallah*" being the operator, would bring a dying man to Mother Teresa's Home and leave him at the front entrance. He would then go to the back entrance and wait in line for the next newly deceased body to be loaded onto his rickshaw and would be given money to take the body to the cremation *ghats*, a place near the Holy River Ganges where bodies were burned. The money would cover the cost of a limited amount of wood for the fire as well as the payment to the rickshaw-*wallah*.

Entering Mother Teresa's Home for the Dying, I walked into a cavernous, high-ceilinged room lit only by stained-glass windows. There was no furniture other than about thirty neatly arranged pallets on the floor. Nuns or volunteers moved quietly among the cadaverous figures on the pallets, none of whom was more than a day from death. The women gave each inert figure a drink of water, perhaps wiped a dirty face and limbs, perhaps applied a little ointment to ease the pain of a sore, but were unable to do more. These men were dying and knew it; it was their duty to accept the small kindnesses that helped ease their passage. Perhaps the most striking thing was the cool, quiet room, in contrast to the hot, noisy temple from which I had just come.

Mother Teresa was not there the day I visited. She was a force of nature, and often made the rounds of businessmen and politicians for donations, and usually got them. When I left, I put all my unneeded cash in the offering container. It was a pittance, but I had to do something.

About a year later, a Turkish friend of mine visited New Delhi as part of a festival of Turkish films. Halit Refiğ was known as the John Ford of Turkey, a masterful storyteller in celluloid. In addition to the festival events, the Indians had arranged a tour of Calcutta for the visiting directors, and I urged Halit to visit the Kali temple and Mother Teresa's. When he returned, he looked chastened: "Dave, I've never seen anything like that in my life, and hope not to again. Once is really enough."

I know what he meant.

On another visit to Calcutta, I decided to walk from our office to the nearby center of the city and found myself in Lord Curzon Park. My staff assured me that I had to see "Rat Park" for myself and refused to explain what that meant.

Named for the British viceroy of India in the early twentieth century, Curzon Park was near the Maidan, one of the few large green spaces left in the central city; Indian families would picnic there on holidays. I strolled through the cool green space, acknowledging greetings and returning smiles, even accepting a small offering of whatever they were having for lunch. Eventually I made my way to nearby Curzon Park, and the busy street on the other side informed me I had come to the end of my calm stroll.

There was a low fence around a small corner, and scurrying about inside the fence were large city rats—not big, cute "Mickey Mice" but wily street-thug rats, a genetic mixture sporting a riot of browns, blacks, and grays—and dirt. Whole extended families of rats had dug holes in the dirt and were undoubtedly more comfortable than the ragpickers I'd seen on the garbage mountain. None seemed to be trying to get out of the enclosure; they knew a good thing when they saw it, especially a plentiful supply of food.

Lined up on the sidewalk that bordered the rat corner were three pushcarts watched by men selling small bags of popcorn for a few *paisas*. Yes, you could feed the rats to your heart's content. In fact, for Hindus it was an act of worship to do so. Figures of Ganesh, the elephant god of prosperity, show him being conveyed by a rat. So in paying homage to the rats, you were also honoring the god who rode him.

While I was standing there, glad that there was even a small barrier between me and the happy rats, an Indian family— mother, father, and a six- or seven-year-old boy—stopped at one of the carts and purchased a bag of popcorn for the boy to throw to the rats. The boy was of mixed minds about this. He wasn't so sure he wanted to lean over the fence and throw the popcorn to the now waiting rats. When he paused, the parents began first to coax him, then moved to ordering him, and finally, speaking in Bengali, sounded like they were berating him for being frightened. I stood about fifteen feet from this family tableau wondering what to do or say that would help and not be seen as interference by the parents.

Finally the boy relented and, overcoming his fear, simply tossed the whole bag into the swarming rats. There was an outburst of squealing as the rats tore into the bag, and in ten seconds not a single piece of popcorn and only a little of the paper bag remained.

Evidently thinking that had been fun, the boy ran back to his parents asking for another bag. They bought it for him, but I surmised, as did he, that this was probably the last one. Again a repetition of the squabbling over the popcorn, and it was over. He glanced at me, and I smiled and gave him a thumbs-up. Having performed his religious duty, he returned to his mother and had his hands carefully wiped, and the family, smiling at me, went on their way.

I felt relieved that my religion does not require me to feed rats, but, on the other hand, perhaps it does. All God's creatures, even the dirty, frightening ones, need a little tangible help at times.

I've already mentioned that the art scene in Calcutta was thriving. One evening, my office staff insisted that I go to the opening of a show by a local artist whom I'll call Tandra.

The first item I saw was a small five-inch pewter sculpture of a mother street dog, like the hundreds that roam Calcutta. In her mouth was what at first looked like a chunk of garbage but on closer inspection proved to be a puppy. The metal mother was frozen in the act of saving or moving one of her pups. This was not Tandra's work, but I quickly purchased it.

Tandra was a painter; her work was reminiscent of the primitive school, and I was very taken by a two-foot-square painting of a Bengali village market. Tandra assured me that this was the view of the market from her apartment kitchen window. I was dubious, but it was possible if her apartment was on the outskirts of the city. I didn't buy a large amount of art abroad, and when I did it was usually something, like the mother street dog, that spoke to me at the moment. I'm not a knowledgeable critic but simply go on what appeals to me.

The pewter dog and Tandra's painting traveled with me to my follow-on tour in Ankara and then were shipped to our home in Montana. The dog has gone "lame": one of her feet has come off the wooden display block, and I have to get it fixed. But the painting now occupies a place of honor on a wall across from the first artwork I ever bought in Athens, a stylized painting of a Greek church.

It's odd how little pieces of your travels always seem to stick to you when they are determined to remain part of your life.

CHAPTER 23

An Introduction to Kemal

Kemal and I looked each other over with mutual curiosity and suspicion. I'm not overly attracted to characters with hair growing out of their ears, and Kemal's small ears were full of short black tufts completely obscuring the openings. His eyes were odd too: unblinking, dark, liquid orbs, bulging out at me from under heavy brows but with very un-ordinary long, gracefully curling eyelashes, at least for a male. His lower lip jutted out farther than the upper one, revealing badly stained teeth, the kind tobacco chewers acquire. His breathing sounded hoarse, strained as though he needed a nasal inhaler, and even from two feet away I could tell he had something against mouthwash. And then there was his size: even kneeling, his eyes gazed directly into mine.

"Hello, Kemal," I muttered.

He said nothing, just continued to gaze with that unblinking stare. Did I imagine it, or did his lip curl in a hint of disdain? I reached out my hand, and he turned his head away, tilting it up and jutting his chin out. He was obviously no more taken with me than I with him. A crowd of small boys had gathered around us, aware that something of interest might happen. I felt their stares and could see several of them making half-hearted attempts to hide childish sneers at my discomfort. I knew I had to act, to take charge of the situation.

"Well!" I said, hoping that the exclamation mark would give me a moral edge. Kemal only gazed and grunted. Adding to my feeling of awkwardness was my attempt not to look at his humped back; I usually try not to let the handicapped know that I find their physical deformity obvious. But try as I might, I couldn't keep from glancing furtively at Kemal's hump glaringly visible behind his head.

A not altogether stifled giggle from the growing crowd of urchins behind me signaled that I had to make my move. Hoping that I looked more firmly purposeful than I felt, I took a step toward Kemal's side, trying to get behind his stare. His gaze followed me, and when, now behind him, I turned, expecting to see no more than his profile, I found him still staring me straight in the face, his whole head and neck having swiveled a complete 180 degrees.

The boys' giggles were obvious now, most of them grinning openly, waiting expectantly as only small boys can for an adult to make an utter ass of himself. Having gone this far, I knew I had to press on, national honor, not to mention my growing mortification, being at stake. I manfully swung my right leg up and over Kemal's back, having to give a little push with my still-earthbound left foot, and found myself unsteadily astride him with my legs dangling awkwardly several inches from the ground.

That seemed to be what Kemal was expecting. With an explosive tracheal eruption somewhere between a belch and groan, he began to rise from the rear. I felt myself simultaneously shoot skyward and begin to pitch forward, my legs flailing wildly to get my feet through a couple of pieces of worn rope that hung from the blanket tied around him. Luckily both toes caught the loops. As my feet and ankles strained from the sinister pull of gravity, I threw my upper torso backward to compensate for the forward pitching motion. My center of gravity teetered at the point of no return, squeals of laughter from the boys confirming my sense that I was on the verge of being tossed headfirst into the sand.

Just as I'd almost given up to that embarrassing certainty, I was violently thrown back in the opposite direction. I struggled to shift my legs and weight, my hands discovering frantically that there was nothing to grasp, for now I was in imminent danger of sliding ingloriously off the back. Somehow my body compensated faster than my mind. and after another smaller lurch forward, I found myself perched seven feet in the air atop the first camel I've known by his given name. The applause from the crowd of boys was good-natured, but there was a hint of disappointment that I had cheated them out of watching a first-timer flatten himself into the desert. Kemal too gave a little snort of disappointment; we both had an uneasy premonition that this might be a long week together.

The journey toward my rendezvous with Kemal had begun at four o'clock on the morning after Christmas, as my wife, Kathleen, I, and our two visiting friends from the States groped our way downstairs and out into a cold and predictably foggy New Delhi morning. By the time we reached the bus that was to take us and ten other masochists from the foreign community out to the desert state of Rajasthan for a weeklong camel safari, we'd woken up enough to join the others in the predictable jokes about the coming sore butts and Ben Gay. Nevertheless, at 5:00 a.m. and at the beginning of an adventure, who's in the mood to argue? The bus rolled out into the morning fog, everyone in high humor.

New Delhi has grown up at the eastern edge of India's Rajasthan desert, a windy stretch of dry country that continues westward into Pakistan and swings south for several hundred miles. The topography ranges from dusty flats to red sand dunes to barren, rocky mountains, but the operative word is dry. Some limited agriculture is possible by either irrigation or yearly monsoon rains, but the crops are those that can do with little water; primarily winter mustard for oil and sesame for seeds. The scattered bright green and yellow patches of mustard and the occasional kitchen garden of cabbages or beans provide a brief visual respite, but the relief from the vast, tired, monochromatic landscape is fleeting. It is, after all, the *karma* of crops to be plucked at their ripe lushness. To this end, all their defenses have been bred out of them; they rely on man's fences or scarecrows to protect them, on man to feed and water them. The scraggly shrubs and trees, anything that grows outside the flimsy fences that discourage foraging animals, seem at first glance to be open to the predations of goats. Little survives below the height of a hungry goat on his hind legs. Wild vegetation, after millennia of being browsed, burnt, cut, and flayed, has learned to fight back by being as unattractive as possible: thistles and thorns, and tiny, waxy, foul-tasting or odiferous leaves all ward off what predators they can, and somehow deep-rooted, spindly, and bristly patches of gray-green, dusty plants and scrub trees survive. Those that do make it to some size grudgingly offer a little shade that attracts men and beasts, from which the trees in turn exact a little nourishment or moisture from the dung or urine excreted at their base. What little they give is still only a means to get.

There are two notable exceptions to this bleak pattern. Wherever the ground water is close enough to the surface, the beautiful *neem* tree thrives. Reminiscent of the American cottonwood, its broad, leafy branches usually mean that water is available from a natural seep or man-dug well. The *neem's* fulsome shade and deep green are welcome respites from the dust and sun.

The other desert-dwelling vegetation that seems to have survived both the elements and man is the *kejari* tree. With a long, deep taproot, it thrives in completely sandy soil, even when there is no apparent water. In the winter, its smaller branches are carefully pruned back, leaving the trunk and larger branches like amputees' stumps silhouetted limbless and leafless against a barren landscape. The small branches are gathered into bundles, loaded on camel carts, and carried to the villages where the leaves are stripped from the twigs and fed to camels and water buffalo. The twigs are dried and burned as fuel or lashed together in the short fences that protect the main food crops and line the borders of a villager's mud hut. In the early summer monsoon, the tree puts out new shoots and leaves and grows madly, making chlorophyll for six months or so before it is again shorn during the dry winter for its fodder. The tree seems to have struck a bargain with man: it is never cut down for firewood, always a tempting possibility when fuel-hungry peasants contemplate a large-trunked tree. In return for being spared, it submits to an annual pruning that yields sustenance for the animals upon which the desert men depend.

We headed toward the northern tip of this area, a region called Shekhawati after one of the fifteenth century Hindu Rajput princes who, when they weren't fighting the Mogul sultans from Delhi, quarreled mightily among themselves. A subcaste of the *Kshatriya*, or warrior caste, the Rajputs consider themselves superior to other warriors as American Marines do to the rest of the military; they are gung-ho fighters, steeped in their own special traditions, succeeding against great odds, and second to none. There didn't seem to be enough elbow room in medieval Rajasthan for all the Rajputs who considered themselves worthy to rule; the history of the area is one of constant fighting and dying.

Our bus driver seemed to have a similar death wish; perhaps he'd been an elephant *mahout* in one of his previous lives, charging into an invading army hoping for a glorious death in battle. Our bus barreled down a rural "highway" barely two lanes wide with shoulders varying in quality from mud ruts to deep sand. The road was an obstacle course of cars, trucks, buses, scooters, bicycles, and animal carts, all moving in different directions at different speeds. We slowed down only to dodge police checkpoints and barricades, road debris, and a variety of slower conveyances creaking along with oversized loads of straw, bricks, pipe, or bottled gas cylinders. One moment we were whizzing along at forty-five miles an hour scattering chickens and peacocks and vultures off the road, then with a wrench of brakes, gears, and horn, we settled in behind a camel cart at five miles an hour. Driving meant one hand on the horn, one on the wheel, a foot on the gas and one on the brake. Potholes or elephant traps, I'm not sure which, carved the driving surface into a neck-wrenching roller-coaster track.

Our driver, however, couldn't compare to the real Rajputs of the Indian roads, the *truckwallahs*, maniacally bent on certain death, piloting killer trucks as they're often referred to. Having little training and even shorter life spans, these swaggering fellows gunned their poorly maintained and usually vastly overloaded vehicles at breakneck speed down whatever passed for a road. They would attempt to overtake and pass anything, and when the vehicle being overtaken was another equally overloaded truck, the two would sweep along side by side for miles, each refusing to give in to the other. Anything that happened to be coming from the other direction had to careen off the side and risk overturning or face certain demolition in a head-on confrontation with the trucks. India is said to have the highest accident rate in the world; a drive along any of its highways will bear that out. In a previous eight-hour trip down and back from the Rajasthani city of Jaipur, we counted twelve truck carcasses "turned turtle," as Indian English puts it.

The *truckwallahs* usually gather to rest at tea houses just off the roads, small establishments that try to entice their clientele to eat their midday rice and *dal* (lentils) by offering free use of one of the dozen or so *charpoys* (rope cots) scattered about. Sometimes these "tea houses" are situated along the open road, sometimes in roadside villages. Wrapped in grimy shawls and turbans, the village men and transient *truckwallahs* huddle around smoky fires of oily engine rags. December is winter and cold in the Indian desert. Pigs and chickens rooted and scratched in the ever-present piles of trash and garbage for whatever the mangy dogs had found inedible. On a cold, gray winter morning, it was a depressing scene.

The larger market towns were usually more densely jumbled versions of the villages; everything that belches or excretes does so, the air the same dirty gray-brown as the tractor fumes, piles of steaming dung, or gobs of coughed-up phlegm. Our bus horn, though it sounded like the Queen Mary lost in a North Atlantic fog, made little impression against a sound-wall of unmuffled trucks, human shouts, animal squeals, scooter beeps, sweatshop machinery, and bike bells.

After nearly nine hours of this exotic scenery, we plowed, clawed, and mauled our way into much drier, sandier, and thus slightly less populated country. Our bus finally ground to a halt in what for the moment seemed like the middle of the desert. There, like a mirage in the late afternoon sunlight, sat our dining tent, a gaily-colored *shamiana* (cotton tarp) resembling a small circus tent enclosed on two sides with fabric "walls." Underneath it, covered tables were set up, aluminum lawn chairs carefully arranged, crockery and stainless neatly in place, and a buffet table laden with steaming rice and curry. So intent were we to get at the food, decorously served by a waiter in white, that we hardly took notice of the horde of children hovering near the tent, or the stately line of camels kneeling in the sand a little distance away. It dawned on us that we were about to mount up for a short end-of-the-day familiarization ride with our camel.

As described, Kemal's and my initial introduction had been a bit traumatic for both. But it was an accurate indicator of the uniqueness of riding a camel. Being a Texan with a certain competence with horses, I had assumed that riding a camel would be at least similar to riding a horse. Both have four legs, yes; one rides on the backs of both, yes. There the similarity ended. Kemal's motion was a simultaneous roll-yaw-pitch, caused by his singular characteristic of moving both his fore and hind legs on the same side at the same time. The horse has the good sense, at least from this rider's viewpoint, to alternate the two: when the left foreleg is extended, the left rear leg is firmly on the ground.

The camel's gait is at least one of the reasons it is known as "the ship of the desert": the sensation of being perched just forward of the hump of a moving camel is similar to being in the crow's nest of a small sailing vessel moving crosswise through a medium swell. One is thrust alternately forward and backward with the motion of the animal's shoulder and back muscles and simultaneously rolls and yaws from side to side as both legs on the same side of the camel leave the ground at the same time. This peculiar motion, plus the sameness of the desert sands, sends signals to the inner ear similar to those that result in seasickness on a ship.

If seasickness were the only hazard, a dose of Dramamine might solve the problem. But a more sinister malady lurked under this exotic undulation. The two cheeks of the rider's buttocks were thrown in frequent and intimate contact. Added to the constant rubbing were sweat, sand, and sometimes an inconveniently located seam of apparel. Predictably, depending on the thickness of one's hide, layers of skin begin to disappear. For those thin-skinned individuals, raw sores were mistaken at first for ordinary muscle ache and only later, upon visual examination by some intimate friend, revealed to be possible sites of infection.

Kathleen developed a cute pair of these saddle sores after the second morning on her camel; my less sensitive rear end took another day and a half to develop the same. When such happens, one has the choice of continuing in suffering silence or asking oneself—rather sensibly—"Why am I paying good money just to be uncomfortable?" If the answer is obvious, then one intelligently joins the tour guide on the camel cart at the end of the file, riding in relative comfort on several thicknesses of cotton padding. If one is fortunate enough to be untroubled by the malady, one stays with it, offering a silent prayer of thanks to the camel gods and occasionally inquiring, with only a slightly condescending touch, after the welfare of those on the cart for the wounded. Of the four of us, Kathleen and I went back to the cart earliest, followed eventually by our first guest, Vicki. Only our second visitor, Marne, rode it out, happily joining the ranks of those who seemed unaffected.

Our first couple of days passed thusly: a cautious testing, attempting to adapt to Kemal's or his cousins' ungainly but efficient gait. Our group of fourteen almost always rode single file, but occasionally one or another of the drivers would get tired of eating the dust or scent of the camel and riders in front and, with a switch on the flanks of his mount and cries of *"Hut! Hut! Hut!,"* move at a trot/lope/gallop to the head of the file. These bursts of speed showed the camel to his best advantage: no other beast or machine could move that rapidly, that easily, that quietly, over such sandy landscape, and certainly not on the poor-quality food that propels these ungainly but oddly graceful beasts. Their huge feet, easily twelve to fourteen inches across on the large male camels, hardly sink into the sand. Their pollution is biodegradable and, in fact, when properly mixed with straw and dried, provides fuel for villagers' cooking fires. They managed heavy loads with minimal complaining, and that most apparent when they were forced either up or down with their riders. Then, the drivers' shouts of *"Ja! Ja!"* mingled with groans and roars of protest as the camels' back knees buckled into the sand, followed by the front. Still, they were much less noisy than the only machine that matches them in mobility, a Jeep, and much cheaper to purchase and maintain. Camels, we were told, are available for five thousand to eight thousand rupees—$300 to $480. The only animal that could come close in durability would be a water buffalo, a bit of an anomaly here in the desert but very much in evidence; however, they are much slower, carry less load, and require more and better fodder than camels. So, in light of the advantages, a few saddle sores could be tolerated.

Being intimately thrown in with these curious creatures for the week, we accumulated a good deal of miscellaneous camel lore, some details more obvious than others. To wit:

- Camels are *big*. At least the ones we saw. Their huge heads seem oversized for the long, arched neck, and even kneeling, a nudge from a mucous-caked nose can send an unsuspecting bystander sprawling. And from the novice's perch atop the hump, it can seem a long six feet to the sand below.
- They seem a chatty bunch, particularly while standing around with nothing much else to do. Sighs, snorts and snuffles, groans, gurgles and belches, lip-smacking and teeth grinding all prove not-so-subtle clues that a group of camels is nearby.
- Male camels pee backward. They are rather strangely designed: when they come to a halt in their march, they spread their rear legs and let loose in that direction from the oddly angled penis under the belly. The stream of urine would thus ordinarily soak the tufts of hair at the end of their tails. For this reason, foresighted camel drivers tie the tails of their mounts around and to the

side of the animal's rump, thus minimizing the chance that a flicking tail will wet down everyone in sight.

- It seems, on the authority of our Rajput guide, that camels can't mate without the assistance of humans because the male's organ is angled the wrong way, Without the assistance of someone holding the female's tail out of the way and guiding in the erect penis, no baby camels are possible. How camels got started in the first place remains a mystery.

There is a myth that explains the camel's anatomy, told to me later by a retired colonel from the Indian camel corps, which patrols the desert near Pakistan.

When God created the animals, He forgot to endow the males with the necessary instrument of reproduction. When He realized the error, He immediately sent out a recall notice advising all the animals to return and pick up their proper equipment. As the animals returned, God reached in a box and presented them with the instrument most appropriate for each according to the animal's size and status: the mice and rabbits got very small ones, the cats and dogs medium size, and so on.

The camel had been out grazing in the desert when the recall notice was sounded and didn't hear about it until late. When he came running in for his organ, God had already passed out almost everything. Only one small, leftover appendage remained in the box, and this He offered with apologies to the camel.

"But Lord," the camel protested: "This is much too small! I'm a very large animal, like the horse or elephant, and I deserve a much larger organ."

"I'm sorry," said God, "but I've given them all away except this one. You'll just have to take it. You must, you know, or there will be no baby camels to continue your line."

"Never!" huffed the camel, and turned to run away.

Peeved by the camel's pride, but knowing that he'd need one of these, God took careful aim at the retreating camel and threw the organ after him, where it stuck facing backward.

And that's the story of how the camel came by his odd endowment.

The camels, however, were still just our means of locomotion through the extraordinary landscape they inhabit. Some of the country through which we rode was typically desert, nothing but sand dunes and *kejari* trees. We slept in tents set up on the sand, but with a couple of thick cotton mattress pads under us, and sleeping bags and heavy cotton quilts to protect us against the desert chill. The hot coffee and tea around a morning fire and the hearty English-style breakfasts under the *shamiana* were comfortable ways to start the day.

During the trip, I occasionally wondered about my search for and pleasure in the innocence or purity of unspoiled villages—our nostalgia for the comforting, supportive "fiddler on the roof" who accompanies Tevye's tribute to tradition. Undoubtedly, there is just as much personal and social heartache and headache in a remote Rajasthani village as anywhere, but there is also a strong sense of identity bred in the unquestioned ruts of following one's social, sexual, and religious role. A kind of deep self-confidence allows the freedom to be openly curious, to stare, to laugh good-naturedly at the oddity of those outside one's own community, and to be hospitable. Those firmly planted in their own social setting can welcome strangers and let them pass; they are less threatened or enticed by the temporary strangeness in their midst.

The probity and innocence of the more remote villages contrasted sadly with the mayhem surrounding our passage through or camping near the larger towns situated near blacktop roads. "Civilization"—electricity, alcohol, television access to the larger and falsely glittery world—had brought with it the predictable breakdown of the restraints of tradition. Here our appearance and camp brought hordes of children, not just curious but hysterical. Less fearful of authority, even the *chowkidars* (watchmen) we hired were unable to keep them from dashing among the tents, pulling at our clothing, shouting epithets. "Youngmen" (as the Indian newspapers refer to them)—lounging adolescent youths—would slouch boldly in the middle of our campsite, puffing on *bidis* (local cigarettes), and swaggering insolently when confronted. We seldom saw adults, and when we did, they were usually attempting to hawk something at an outrageous price.

The main reason we visited the larger towns at all was to see the *havelis* built in or near them. These large traditional villas had been built over the last hundred years or so by a group or class of local inhabitants called Mawaris, those coming from Mawar, a subregion of Rajasthan. Simultaneously reviled and envied for their sharp business practices and their single-minded devotion to making money, the Mawari families had prospered as merchants on the old trade routes through Rajasthan between Persia and northern India to the east and south. They later migrated to the great commercial cities of India—Calcutta and Bombay—where they became the wealthiest of the controlling interests in those cities. But they built villas in their hometowns that reflected their newly acquired status. A unique architectural style, the mansions evolved around courtyards that provided security for the family and privacy for the women as well as protecting the inhabitants from the long, harsh summers. Today they stand abandoned except for the family watchman, who sleeps on the property, still owned but rarely used by the descendants of the now distant families who built them. Ornately frescoed, with finely carved wooden doors and shutters, lavishly decorated with marble and corroded brass, the pompous rooms now house only pigeons and mice.

Perhaps this is why I feel sad, even uneasy, with these dusty, monumental reminders of former glories. There seems so little connection with the present, so little attempt to integrate the sense of past and present. On the last night of our trip, for example, we stayed in a "restored" palace hotel in the seventeenth century town of Nawalgarh. The owners had attempted to add electricity and plumbing, but rusty pipes and exposed wiring had been fastened helter-skelter on the outside of the walls. The fabric used to upholster moldy, overstuffed chairs ranged from dusty, reused silk brocade to modern Mickey Mouse and Donald Duck printed cotton. Locally embroidered bedspreads covered beds of wooden planks softened only by thin cotton padding. Halls that were once filled with ornately carved wooden furniture now boasted only rusty folding metal chairs. A cuisine that once prided itself on the delicacy of its flavors has now fallen to gristly mutton or bony chicken, stewed to death in its own gravy, and rice. And for me, the ultimate hypocrisy was the folk dances performed the last evening for the tourists, in which seductively whirling transvestites mimicked the woman's part of a traditional village dance. I learned later that most of them were eunuchs, an entire caste of these people—*hijras*—trying to earn a meager living in a culture of nonacceptance.

India is impossible to distill. There is no single essence of the land and people, no trademark image like Swiss alpine travel-poster purity or American canyonland vastness. The mind's eye isn't wide enough; the images and sensations of any single experience here are, perhaps as they can be only in India, jumbled, chaotic, and mixed. Our fascination with camels was tempered by the uncomfortable reality of saddle sores. Mingling with the innocent curiosity of the more remote village children was the sullen dark side of the neighboring town rowdies. The skies were still clear in the desert but difficult to see in the towns. We came home laden with the memories of colors and sounds: bright yellow and green Rajasthani *saris* against red mud walls; a pink and saffron sky at sunset; the camels' multicolored tack and harnesses; peacocks' blue and turquoise tails in full, proud display; camels' bells and bellows; the raucous cries of crows and the rustle of eucalyptus; friendly village laughter and the chatter of our drivers' desert dialect.

Kemal and I did not, in the end, prove to be the best of friends, but he provided me with a unique perspective—literally and figuratively—on Rajasthan. Sometimes heady, much of the time difficult, almost always strange, one seems always at the beginning in India.

CHAPTER 24

Landing in New Delhi: Wheels Up or Wheels Down?

Each city in which we had branch offices was unique: Bombay was the commercial center of India, Calcutta was a world of its own, and Madras seemed like a southern town with a slower pace and an interesting mix of the major religions of India, including Thomasine Christianity. I visited these cities every couple of months and became intimately acquainted with Indian Airlines flights to and from each. One trip coming back to New Delhi from Madras remains a vivid memory.

I had finished my visit and decided to take an early evening flight back to Delhi, so I could sleep in my own bed. The plane departed as usual about 7:00 p.m. with an expected arrival time of 9:00 p.m. Since I'd learned not to trust the assumption that checked luggage would make it on the same plane as I traveled, I always carried a small shoulder bag with a change of clothes, a few energy bars, and a bottle of water in case of delays.

The flight went smoothly for the first hour. It was a winter night with an early sunset, so the view outside the plane's windows soon showed only the lights of small towns. I busied myself writing up my trip report and reading a book and, in the process, lost track of time. When I finally looked at my watch I could see in the distance the lights of New Delhi. I checked them fifteen minutes or so later, noticing that we seemed to be going toward the lights from a slightly different direction than usual. About the same time I noticed a new sound; the whir of the electric motors under the wings, which I knew from experience was the sound of the motors lowering the landing gear.

The motors would run with a high-pitched sound, then stop, and after a couple of minutes start up again with a lower-pitched noise. It sounded as if the pilots were warming up the landing gear mechanisms, but we were still fifteen or twenty minutes from the lights of the Delhi airport. Finally the motor sounds stopped, so I assumed that whatever had prompted them to turn them on had been addressed.

We continued on our flight path for another fifteen minutes, and then, looking out in the darkness, I had a slight sensation that the plane was not quite horizontal, and the same airport lights kept reappearing in a periodic manner that made me realize that we were flying in a huge circle around and around the outskirts of the city. And we were maintaining the same altitude.

Why would we be doing this? As we continued our large looping circle, it finally dawned on me that perhaps the pilots were trying to use up excess fuel. And the only reason I could think of for that was that there was a possibility we were going to have to land in some unusual way that might cause a crash and a possible fire.

If that was the problem, I would expect the pilots to let the passengers know to prepare for a possible belly landing. However, they offered no explanation.

After continuing this holding pattern for another half hour, I heard the click of the speakers, and the pilot somberly announced, "Ladies and gentlemen, I apologize for the delay in landing, but ground control has had some problems with diverting another incoming aircraft. That has now been solved, and we are cleared to land. I have asked the cabin crew to prepare the aircraft for landing."

The stewardesses made their rounds of the plane, taking special care to see that everyone had their seatbelts tightly buckled and clearing the floor space of briefcases and bags, the usual procedures but carried out with a different level of intensity. I looked around but saw no hint of concern on my fellow passengers' faces.

We now began our actual descent, the pressure in my ears confirming that we were indeed coming down. Then I heard the electric motors again. While I could not see the landing gear under the wing, it definitely sounded like the motors were moving the landing gear into position, only to stop and reverse. I stopped a passing stewardess and asked her whether there was a problem. "Oh no, sir. The pilots just want to exercise the hydraulic systems on the underside of the aircraft."

That sounded as forced as the frozen smiles on their faces, but by this time we were approaching the runway. The cabin crew disappeared to buckle themselves in their shoulder restraints.

The plane crossed the striped lines painted on the far end of the runway, and very, very slowly dropped toward the tarmac. The touchdown was exceptionally gentle, and I noticed that instead of reversing the engines to slow the aircraft more quickly, the pilot seemed to be applying the brakes alone. Coming in at that speed we needed all the runway length he could squeeze out to slow the plane without using the more jarring engine reverse method. But we had no trouble coming to a slower taxi speed and made our way toward the terminal. People began to gather their carry-on items, but whenever one of them tried to stand up and open the overhead compartments, a crew member would sternly order him to sit down and remain buckled in until the plane came to a complete stop.

We finally stopped, and passengers lined up to deplane at the front exit doors. As I got to the door, I noticed a squadron of fire trucks had surrounded the plane. "What's going on, miss?" I asked the young woman at the door.

"Oh, just a ground crew drill, sir. They practice these frequently." If it was a drill, it was certainly realistic: firemen in full protective gear stood holding high-pressure hoses, foam dripping from the nozzles.

I boarded the bus that transported passengers to the terminal, noticing that we had parked much farther than usual from the reception areas. As I got off the bus and went in, I spotted Arun, the embassy expediter, in the crowd of relatives awaiting passengers. This was unusual: Arun didn't usually meet domestic flights, but I was glad to see him.

"Arun! What are you doing here? And what was going on with this flight? We must have circled the city for an hour before landing."

"I'll explain in the morning, Mr. Grimland. We'll get no answers tonight. I see that you don't have any luggage. Shall we get you home to bed? I'll make a call in the morning to a friend of mine in the Indian Airlines office and let you know."

I was tired and recognized that Arun was right. There would be no dependable information at this point.

I slept well that night and was a half hour late getting into the office the next morning. Going straight to Arun's office, I asked him whether he'd learned anything.

"You wouldn't believe this, sir, but my friend tells me on a strictly confidential basis that they couldn't get the landing gear down at first. The plane was just short of the runway when the cockpit indicator confirmed that the gear was down and locked, but it was flickering, so the pilots couldn't be sure."

I was stunned. "But, Arun, they never mentioned the possibility of a landing in those conditions. People should have been told so they could prepare to get out other emergency exits!"

"Ah, my friend tells me that experience has shown that everyone panics if they think there may be a crash. They all want their carry-on luggage with its money or illegal booze in it, and the plane turns into a madhouse and a greater danger than if people simply sit quietly."

I stared at him. "So you mean that we could have all faced instant cremation and a quick move to our next round of reincarnation?"

"Strange things happen to people's logic in this kind of situation," Arun said. "We all think we would like to die quickly, but when we have time to think about it, the choice may not be so clear."

Feeling a little chastened by Arun's response, I said, "You're right, I guess. It looks like one or more of your Hindu gods had his eye on us. Perhaps you'd better explain to me how to figure out which one was responsible and how to properly thank him or her."

Arun smiled. "Sure, sir. But you have to approach the gods with a glass of really good wine in your stomach, and an extra glass for the god."

"I think I could do that, Arun, but we'll have to practice."

"Certainly, sir. I don't usually drink alcoholic beverages, but as long as my boss requests my assistance in learning about the gods, I think it would be okay."

CHAPTER 25

Speaking Truth to Power

During my nearly thirty years in the foreign service, I didn't go looking for situations in which to appear stubborn, but when I found them slapping me in the face I usually spoke up. In a hierarchical organization such as the foreign service, the most difficult experiences were those occasions where an ambassador had his own agenda and, usually for reasons of ego, had no interest in hearing any of his staff's opinions that did not coincide with his. A staffer who chose to voice an unsupportive opinion usually found himself professionally frozen out of future discussions or, in the worst cases, had a snide remark inserted by the ambassador into his annual performance review. Bureaucratic punishment, therefore, was more insidiously effective in ensuring group-think than being keel-hauled as in earlier days.

I served under nine regularly assigned ambassadors, and when one of the best was assassinated in Cyprus, we got two temporary replacements before the president and Senate approved a new accredited man to run the mission.

One of these temporary substitutes in Cyprus used to take a small coterie of embassy folk to northern Cyprus, then controlled by the Turkish army, on "picnics" for a day's R&R after the Greeks had run south during the invasion. In reality these were trips during which the ambassador would go into empty houses and steal folk art—lovely carved bread-making bowls, homemade tools or implements, and household religious icons. His plan was to put them in his diplomatic shipment out of the country, then use them to decorate his own Washington home.

After the first trip, during which I kept my mouth shut, I went into his office and said, "Jim, this is outrageous theft. You know it, and I know it. Either it stops, or I request an immediate transfer—and will take it as public as I can."

He tried to argue—"I'm just 'saving' these little things. The Greeks will never come back, and the stuff will gradually disappear to casual looters."

I didn't try to continue the argument. I just repeated what he knew to be the obvious. And I added, "Everyone who goes on these 'picnics' knows what you're doing; it won't be long before word gets back to somebody in the State Department's inspector's office. And frankly, if someone else doesn't report it to Washington, I will."

He stopped the "picnics," and I stayed.

***

My first ambassador in Bangladesh desperately wanted to accept the American navy's offer to fly out with a group of senior Bangladeshi military officers for an overnight visit of a US carrier in the Bay of Bengal. He brought it up in a special meeting to which he called all the embassy section heads. He went around the room, and everyone—knowing what the ambassador wanted—agreed that it would be okay, until he got to me. I felt strongly that it would be a public relations disaster and explained why: no American carrier had been in the Bay of Bengal since the War of Independence in 1971—a move that was remembered with ill will by the Bangladeshis, who saw it as an attempt to aid West Pakistan in its domination of East Pakistan. To revive those memories in Bangladesh now, just for the sake of giving our ambassador and a few generals an ego trip to the carrier, would be stupid and counterproductive.

The ambassador simply didn't want to hear my argument. With no further ado, he angrily adjourned the country team meeting with the explanation, "Well, I can see that everyone favors my visit except the PAO. I suppose that kills it."

I returned to my office and waited for the inevitable call, which finally came late in the day. The ambassador was standing at a window looking out, a grim expression on his face. Never looking at me, he said, "Well, you knew what I wanted this morning, and you still spoke up. And you were right. I'll see to it that I write that in your annual performance report." And he did. That report was what pushed me into the senior foreign service.

Sometimes a senior officer will actually take a few minutes to ponder what has happened and realize his mistake. I've always admired this particular ambassador for doing exactly that—and for going out of his way to see that my contribution had been officially noted. It was rare in our business.

***

Six years later, in 1991, I was reassigned to Turkey, this time as country PAO in Ankara, with responsibilities for branch posts in Istanbul and Izmir. I hadn't been there long when my secretary informed me that the ambassador's office had called and an "urgent" country team meeting was starting in ten minutes. Ambassadors generally held a weekly meeting of what is called the Embassy Country Team, a group of men (yes, we were all males in those not-so-long-ago days), who met weekly with the ambassador to brief him and the rest of the group on what our sections were doing.

When I arrived, the embassy's defense attaché was about to speak. "Gentlemen, we've got a problem."

Readers may remember that in 1991 Soviet President Gorbachev had "cut the reins" on the various former Soviet republics, making them independent countries. It was the only choice he had; the Central Asian republics were pulling out on their own anyway. One of these was Kazakhstan, the former Soviet republic on whose territory the Russians had, against the Kazaks' will, tested a nuclear weapon in 1949. The Soviets still used it as a nuclear test facility as well as building and running another facility to enrich and store uranium. The Kazaks had allowed the Russians to retrieve much of the enriched uranium and even dismantle most of the test facility, but the Russians still stored a small amount of nuclear material there, and the Kazaks were afraid that they would tempted to violate Kazakhstan's newfound sovereignty and try to take the material back. So they had secretly asked the United States to send in large cargo planes and remove it for temporary safekeeping to the United States.

Evidently on the morning our meeting was taking place in Ankara, a giant American C-5A cargo plane, the world's largest, had flown into a military base in Kazakhstan to load the radioactive material in its heavy lead-shielded containers. The plane had taken off a little late but was now flying southwest. The plan was for it to fly to Turkey, land at the American-controlled air base at Incirlik in southern Turkey to refuel and then proceed to Spain for a second refueling prior to crossing the Atlantic for the last leg to the United States.

Shortly after the C-5A had taken off, however, it dawned on someone—either on the plane or at Incirlik—to wonder whether the runways at Incirlik were long enough for this heavily laden cargo plane to land and take off again. Incirlik had runways and fuel, but it was used exclusively for fighter aircraft and small supply cargo planes, not multiton C5A's loaded with enriched uranium. One would think this question might have been asked before, but the US military is no different than any other bureaucracy and simply missed checking this minor (?) detail. Anyway, this was not the time to find someone to blame. The US plane's pilot was about two hours from needing to land in Turkey. Where was he supposed to go?

The defense attaché had quickly researched the only other possibility, which unfortunately was the international civilian airport in Ankara. In ninety minutes, this plainly US-marked behemoth needed to land there—in broad daylight. The Turks would not be happy to have an American military aircraft clearly visible on Turkish soil, especially because the Turkish government would have to be told about the cargo. Yes, we did have a problem.

After some desultory discussion about what to do, I pointed out that the Turkish newspapers and state television station maintained a few reporters, photographers, and cameramen at the Ankara airport on a 24/7 basis. When this plane landed, someone would see and photograph it as it pulled up to the refueling hoses. The embassy was going to be flooded with telephone calls from the press, as was the Turkish government, and no one knew for sure whether the Turkish government had been told of the problem. What was going to be our response?

Our ambassador then made what had to be the dumbest remark heard in that conference room during its entire existence. "Well, Grimland, if reporters call, tell 'em it's dog food. The plane's carrying dog food to our bases in Europe."

My god, I thought, *does he really believe that we'd get away with an idiotic lie?* The looks from others around the table indicated they were thinking the same thing.

Drawing a deep breath, I formulated a more diplomatic response than I felt.

"First, Mr. Ambassador, Turkish newsfolk are no dumber than their American counterparts. Telling them it's dog food will only set us up for first hilarious, then angry responses in tomorrow's headlines."

"Second, sir, the only way I can be an effective spokesman is to keep my reputation for being truthful. I can get better cooperation by saying 'No comment,' or 'I'll get back to you on that.' But if I use this dog food response, nothing I say in the future will be believed."

"To hell with your morals, man, and to your fear of losing your spokesman's virginity. *Just do it!*"

"Shouldn't we be sure, sir, whether the Turkish government has been told of this emergency? It seems to me that they should be in on the real story and that we should coordinate our response with theirs."

Fortunately at this point, John, the embassy political officer, spoke up. "I agree with Dave, sir. To my knowledge, the Turks have not been notified—this has all happened too fast. I suggest that I get in touch with the Turkish Foreign Ministry and tell them of our problem as well as asking for their cooperation. I'm sure they'll want to alert their crisis management folk too. After all, as good as our pilots are, they are carrying an extremely hazardous load, and, God forbid, if we have a bad landing or something else that causes even a small radiation leak, they'll want to have their teams of people handy. That will increase the visibility of the whole thing and make it a mutual public affairs crisis instead of just a diplomatic one. I should think they would be anxious to work with us."

I was relieved. Someone else had jumped in and provided a way out of a head-on collision between me and the ambassador. I chimed in, "As soon as John has passed the word to the Turks, sir, I'll call on the Ministry of Foreign Affairs press spokesman and agree on a public response. But we'd better get moving—the clock isn't stopping for us."

"Well, I can see we've got a bunch of nervous nellies," grunted the ambassador. Why is it almost always necessary for people who think they're in command to put down anyone who has a better idea? At some level, they just don't understand that anyone should do anything except salute and say, "Yes, sir."

We broke up. John phoned his contact at the Foreign Ministry, and I phoned mine, telling them both we had to come see them on an urgent errand. We went first to John's appointment, and, while concerned, the official was understandably more worried about the unlikely possibility of a nuclear accident than he was about a little negative press publicity. He promised to call the press spokesman to brief him while we walked over to the nearby building where his office was. We were shown in immediately.

"Good morning, Mr. Ersoy, I gather you've already been brought up to speed on why we're here." Just to be sure, I went over the facts quickly.

"Indeed, Mr. Grimland, and we appreciate what I think you Americans call 'being in on the takeoff instead of just the crash landing.'" I wasn't sure his analogy was quite apt in this case but didn't tell him so. "So what do you suggest, sir, by way of a common response to the press?"

He leaned back in his chair. "I don't think we have to have a response, Mr. Grimland. There simply won't be a story or even a mention of this in the press or state TV."

Startled, I asked him why.

"Because I will simply make a few phone calls to certain persons in the papers and state television, and I guarantee that nothing will be reported, short of a major crisis on landing. I gather you Americans are not too worried about that? We too have nuclear facilities close to civilian populations, and we've learned both to prepare for it and live with it. Fortunately, with anything short of a major crash by the C-5A, small radiation leaks will be blown by the prevailing west wind and dissipate in the atmosphere long before they are a danger to anyone. But

I think I can guarantee you, sir, that there will be no media coverage of a normal landing."

While I remembered this kind of control in the early 1980s when the Turkish military ran the country, I had no idea the current civilian government could be so sure of its control of the often rambunctious private newspapers.

"Again, thank you for your concern, Mr. Grimland. By the way, can you tell me who came up with this ingenious 'dog food' line?"

I have no idea how he'd heard of that and knew he wouldn't tell me.

"Well, sir, it was a remark made as a joke by someone."

He smiled: "Ah, yes, we too have our 'jokers.' Sometimes we don't know whether to laugh or cry."

Needless to say, Mr. Ersoy was right. The American "dog food" plane landed at the Ankara airport without incident and refueled in an hour. Conveniently, no civilian aircraft carrying tourists or businessmen landed—they were somehow inexplicably delayed before they left the airports from which they were scheduled. Our plane was off to Spain without anyone bringing it up. I could only hope the Spaniards would be as effective.

Had this incident bent the democratic rules of freedom of speech? Perhaps, just a little. But no one had been seriously delayed making his or her flight connections in Ankara, and a larger good had been accomplished by getting the uranium out of Kazakhstan. All in all, it wasn't a bad day's work.

AFTERWORD

The Road to Ithaka Continues: Islam in Plentywood, Montana

When I insist that my *Journey to Ithaka* continues, I quite literally mean that. My experiences with Muslims, which came out of my foreign service years, were useful in bringing that information to audiences all over Montana, when I retired in 1995 to Columbus, Montana.

In 2003, the United States started beating the drums of war to go in and rid Iraq of our ally-become-tyrant Saddam Hussein. Part of any war effort is the necessity of demonizing one's enemy, and as Americans hitched up their pants and loaded their guns, I began to hear media reports of our political leaders describing Saddam as a murderous, lying Muslim, the clear implication being that Saddam's religion was the evil moral basis of his political action.

None of this bombastic rhetoric fit Islam as I had experienced it in Cyprus, Turkey, Bangladesh, or India. Saddam's twisted *politics*, not his religion, allowed him to kill his fellow Muslims, whether they were Kurds, Shiites, or Sunnis. Even after the horror of the World Trade Center attacks in 2001, most

Americans still knew little about the history and tenets of the world's fastest-growing religion.

I was disturbed enough to respond to an invitation from the Columbus High School adult education program and offer a series of weekly talks and discussions with whomever signed up to learn about Islam on five consecutive cold winter nights. About a dozen folks signed up, and when the planned five evenings were over, the group voted to keep on with another five nights. Based on the success of the high school adult education program, I applied for and was accepted by Humanities Montana as one of its subsidized speakers. I then began planning my first long trip around the northeast corner of Montana for a series of public presentations sponsored by libraries and small colleges. About the same time, the local county library invited me to do a single evening lecture on Islam. That program was written up by a *Billings Gazette* reporter who happened to live in Columbus.

Unbeknownst to me, the *Los Angeles Times* correspondent in Seattle, Sam Verhovek, regularly scanned regional papers in the far northwestern states, and the day after the story on my library talk appeared in the *Billings Gazette*, Sam called and asked if he could come and cover a similar story in a rural setting. Since I had planned to visit the Fort Peck Sioux-Assiniboine reservation college in Wolf Point, I found another sponsor in Plentywood, even farther north, and suggested that Sam cover either or both of those presentations. He agreed and flew to Billings, after arranging for a New York-based Pulitzer Prize-winning photographer, Carolyn Cole, to meet us in Fort Peck. From there we all drove to Plentywood, watching the February weather reports of a pending Canadian cold air mass invading the area. The photographer had to get a flight back before weather socked her in, but Sam and I drove on up to the Canadian border, where the Plentywood library had advertised a single talk at the courthouse. Besides the blizzard coming in—it was already windy with light snow falling and the time and temperature sign on the local bank read twelve degrees—the sponsoring library had scheduled my talk on the same night as an important local basketball game. All in all, competition for an audience was pretty intense. I was surprised when fifty hardy souls turned up for two hours of discussion about Islam.

Interestingly, when I began my talk in Plentywood that night, I asked, as I usually did, whether there were any Muslims in the audience and invited them to express any differing views on what I was going to say about Islam. In the case of Plentywood, I did so out of form rather than a real expectation of anyone raising his hand.

This time, however, I was the one who was surprised. A young high school-aged lad held up his hand and in excellent English introduced himself

"I am Alishar Taylanzoda from Tajikistan."

In talking to him and his host family afterward, I learned that the local school had offered itself as an exchange location to an organization that arranged high school student exchanges. And the school had even asked for a Muslim boy. Most of the people in Plentywood, forty miles south of the Canadian border and 120 miles from the nearest mosque in Regina, had probably never heard of Tajikistan, never traveled to central Asia, and were unlikely to do so in the future. But the northeastern corner of Montana has long had a reputation as a liberal dot in this largely conservative state. Alishar's presence in their town had given them a reason to brave the beginning blizzard as well as forego the community's sports event to come listen to someone they'd never heard of, a man who lived six hundred miles from Plentywood, talk about Islam.

We took an intermission for coffee and cookies, and during the break, Sam Verhovek was doing his journalist thing, talking to people and getting halftime impressions.

I overheard him talking to a steely-eyed woman of about fifty, pretty obviously a rancher's wife. Sam listed the sources of news available in Plentywood: the *Billings Gazette*, TV, Canadian radio, and the Internet. Why would people come out on such a night to hear a retired diplomat they didn't know talk about Islam?

The woman responded, "Listen, mister, out here, we like to sniff the sources of our information."

She and her cowboy-booted husband went on to say that they had some concerns about opening up our country to welcome a bunch of Iraqi Muslims after the war, which was still going on at that time.

"But that don't mean we don't need to know something about them and their religion," she said.

I was sorry that Sam or his editors didn't use the part about Montanans "sniffing" their sources of information—perhaps they thought it sounded too cute. I was quite proud of my fellow Montanans. In spite of hard lives and very few amenities, many rural people here retain a hopeful native curiosity about a world that seems far away.

Remembering my USIS days when I believed that student exchanges were one of our most important tools in helping keep people's minds open, I could imagine that young Alishar Taylanzoda would make a more informed and friendlier future possible, maybe even as Tajik president some day, because of his experience in Plentywood.

These stories happen everywhere in a state more thought of as "Marlboro Man" country than plugged in to the outside world. When the United States was seized, for the wrong reasons, with going into Afghanistan a decade or so ago, my seventy-year-old neighbor rancher called me up one evening and said, "Dave, can you tell me what's all this fuss about Af-a-ghan-is-tan?" And then he listened for almost an hour to my extemporaneous reply, with pauses only for his good questions.

There are interesting people like the rancher's wife and my neighbor all over the world.

If we listen with the same openness to them as we hope they do to us, there's gold to be found in their conversation and interests.

NOTES

Chapter 1: I arrived in my first post, Athens, Greece, in 1968. My first year there was spent in rotational duty as a trainee, learning what different sections in USIS and the Embassy did. When I completed this training, I was assigned as the assistant cultural affairs officer.

A couple of years later, in 1971, I was transferred to Cyprus as the assistant PAO in a two-officer post. The post's public affairs officer transferred out early. I was made the PAO during a period that began with a visit by Secretary of State Henry Kissinger and went on to include a violent Greek Cypriot coup, a Turkish invasion, and the assassination of our ambassador. As a result of the suddenly dangerous conditions, nonessential members of the staff and our families were evacuated, first to Beirut, Lebanon, and then, when Beirut turned violent in 1975, to Europe or the United States.

At the end of my tour there, I was granted a two-year leave without pay to consider whether I wanted to continue in the foreign service. The two years included a year at Pendle Hill, a Quaker Study Center, near Philadelphia, Pennsylvania, that broadened my intellectual and spiritual horizons and ended with my return to the foreign service. In Washington, I was assigned to USIA's Motion Picture and Television Division in charge of coming up with ideas for films that we could either purchase or produce on life in America.

In 1980 I got my chance to return abroad with an assignment to Istanbul, Turkey, as our branch PAO, preceded, of course, by the requisite torture of nine months of intensive training in the Turkish language. After three years, I returned to Washington for a brief stint as executive assistant to the deputy director of USIA. The director of USIA was a political appointee, but the deputy director was a senior FSO. By my choice, this lasted only a few months. I was disgusted by the "view from the top."

I asked to take a much less prestigious position as the deputy director of our Training Division, with primary responsibility for designing and leading the initial nine-week orientation for FSOs just entering the service. This was probably the most professionally and personally enjoyable assignment I had in my career, working with five or six classes of twenty mature adult trainees, many of whom became lifelong friends. I learned that I had teaching skills, at least when the students were mature, motivated learners.

This was followed by a three-year assignment as PAO in Dhaka, Bangladesh, from 1987 to 1990. I then became deputy PAO in New Delhi, India, the largest USIS post in the world, with some thirty American FSOs and about three hundred FSNs in four Indian cities. That assignment lasted four years before I returned to Turkey as country PAO in Ankara, with branch posts in Istanbul and Izmir. I retired in 1995 and moved to Montana, where I continue to live.

More USIA officers were generally given more intensive language training than other FSOs before we left Washington, primarily because we were expected to deal more with contacts whose English was less fluent. And nothing helps one truly understand a culture more than submersing oneself in the language. The subtleties of verbal expression are often crucial to how we think and make decisions. Knowing the formulaic expressions used by Greeks or Turks or Bangladeshis is important to support the feeling of your interlocutor that "this guy understands me" and knows the right way to be respectful. Furthermore, because our USIS posts abroad employed the largest number of foreign service national employees, we had to learn better management skills than many of the other embassy FSOs. Finally, our local Turkish, Indian, or Bangladesh contacts meant that we did a lot more socializing and were often more intimately acquainted with a wider variety of professionals, artists, and intellectuals.

There were certainly frustrations in working for a bureaucracy: writing reams of reports and planning papers that were probably were never read, dealing with ego-driven superiors, and especially working as control officers for the visits of American congressmen who wasted no time trying to impress both their local hosts and us of their superiority. But my years in the foreign service were truly an education in the best sense of the word: living in a country; meeting the most interesting people in that culture, from shepherds to university presidents; being able to communicate with them in their language was—and remains—a rewarding experience.

Chapter 4: The battle of Thermopylae occurred in 480 BC. The Spartans were the main force in the coalition of Greek city-states that sent troops to hold the Persian army at bay, and they had chosen to defend a narrow mountain pass through which the Persian army would have to pass to continue its invasion of Greece. The Greek coalition was under the command of Leonidas, a Spartan general. Sparta was a militaristic society, known for its superb training, disciplined fighting form, and honor-bound determination either to win or die. Young Spartan soldiers were bade good-bye by their parents when they left to do battle, and the last words they heard were the stern admonition: "Come home carrying your shields, or being borne on it." Retreat was not an option. The people we later call "Spartans" were known at the time as "Lacedaeomians."

Ephialtis was a Greek traitor, not a Spartan, who showed the Persian army, with a large contingent of Medes, possibly the ancestors of today's Kurds, a mountain path around the hastily thrown-up barrier that crossed the ancient road through which the invading army would have to pass. The Persians were thus able to go around the Spartans and attack them from the rear at the same time that the main army attacked from the front. Although they quickly understood that they were doomed, the Spartans fought on until the last man had been killed.

The battle and death of the "Spartan 300" was similar in Greek history to the battle of the Alamo and the death of its small force of Texicans. Near the site of the Greek defeat at Thermopolis is a modern life-sized statue of the Spartan General Leonidas in full armor, his bronze horse-hair crested helmet as lifelike as if he was standing there. The inscription on its base reads:

Go, Stranger, and tell the Lacedaemonians that
we lie here in obedience to their laws.

No one has ever caught the spirit of Thermopylae as well as Constantine Cavafy, the early twentieth century Greek poet, in his poem "Thermopylae:"

And even more honor is due to them
When they foresee (as many do foresee)
That Ephialtis will turn up in the end,
That the Medes will break through after all.

Chapter 5: The Byzantines were the first to discover many of the sites considered holy by subsequent Christians. The Wikipedia entry on the Church of the Holy Sepulcher is useful to acquaint oneself with the discovery and history of the site where Jesus was crucified and resurrected. Like so many later Christian sites, the area where the present church sits was formerly a temple to a pagan god or goddess, in this case Aphrodite.

By the Victorian era, the traditions I have described were already well established. But visiting British and American pilgrims doubted that the sites were accurate, and German scholars decided that their interpretation of the geography of first century Jerusalem was more accurate. They found an old Jewish tomb outside the city walls (complete with a skull-shaped hill which had to be Golgotha) and decided this must be the true place where the central events of Christianity took place nearly two thousand years earlier. This site has since been called "The Garden Tomb."

http://en.wikipedia.org/wiki/Garden_Tomb

Chapter 14: While I noted earlier that I'd had no foreign service training in handling extreme nervousness, I doubt that any training course would have done more than warn me not to bolster my confidence with alcohol. Some training officer would have simply noted that getting tipsy would improve neither my judgment nor my social skills. That should have already been apparent from my childhood experience around parents who got drunk quickly and then thought themselves the life of the party.

So exercising a little maturity and judgment would probably have been a better solution to my feelings of awkwardness. I think I learned my lesson, and indeed I never again, in my remaining two decades in the diplomatic service, chose the easy way out—or dirtied another camel's hair sport coat.

Chapter 15: Historically, the Iranians had further reason to distrust the actions and motives of foreigners, particularly the British, Americans, and Soviets. At the beginning of World War II in 1941, Britain and the USSR invaded Iran. The Soviets wanted Iranian oil to fight the Germans, and the British wanted to use the Iranian railroad network to move supplies and troops from British India to battlefronts in Africa and Europe. In the face of Iranian political and military weakness, the British did so without bothering to get Iranian concurrence.

A decade later, the British wanted unimpeded access to Iranian oil, which had originally been developed by British Petroleum. There was a clear imperial assumption that Iranian oil "belonged" to Britain.

The Iranians, however, now led by Prime Minister Mohammed Mosadegh, an immensely popular and freely elected leader, were a fly in the ointment of British ambitions. British intelligence insisted that Mosadegh, who was going to nationalize British Petroleum, had to go. Winston Churchill considered him a "dangerous socialist" (meaning "communist" in the Cold War rhetoric of the early 1950s) and wanted him removed but did not wish to take all the political heat. Instead, Churchill convinced US President Dwight Eisenhower to order the CIA to get rid of Mosadegh.

So in 1953, the CIA, acting on "cooked" British intelligence, organized a coup that ended with Mosadegh's removal from power. This was the first time in its history that the United States had overthrown an elected civilian government. The incident angered the Iranians then and has rankled ever since.

Chapter 17: (1) Bangladesh was part of the British India colony for hundreds of years. When the British left the subcontinent in 1947, East Bengal with Dhaka as its capital was clear across the state of India but became part of Pakistan since it had a Muslim majority. West Bengal with Calcutta as its capital was given to India. Bangladesh, formerly East Pakistan, won its independence from Pakistan in 1971 after a bloody revolution.

(2) A clarification and an apology for a storyteller's exaggeration to those of my former Bangladeshi staff who are still living and may remember something of these incidents. These stories are all true. But in several of those I've written, including this one, I have taken the storyteller's prerogative of inserting details that happened in a different time or occasion. All details are indeed true, but may not have happened in the setting I'm describing. For example, my secretary, Farida Kauser, would not have accepted an invitation for me on the day of my arrival; she was too much of a professional. In fact, I nominated her for and she received an award as "Best Secretary in USIS in the World." She would not have let herself be wheedled by an organization into scheduling me for anything after twenty hours in flight status. Nor would I have been taken to my new house alone, without someone there to greet me, introduce me to the household servants, and show me the basic ropes. I would indeed be uncomfortable for some months with the servants picking out things for me to wear, but that's a little sidebar story that would not stand on its own, so I've incorporated it into this piece where it still lives and breathes with freshness and underlying honesty.

Chapter 21: Dum Dum airport?" you wonder. How did it get that name?

"Dum Dum" was named after the Calcutta suburb that grew up around a munitions factory built by the British in the nineteenth century to produce bullets for the Zulu wars in southern Africa. These were either bullets with a soft lead tip, or later, a hollow tip, that flattened out on impact, causing a much more serious wound. Zulu warriors would get so high on battle fever, helped by chewing a local intoxicant, that they would charge right through the usual British volleys with solid-point ammunition and take terrible wounds from conventional ammunition but keep on coming. The hollow-point rifle bullet was much more deadly, stopping any charging warrior in his tracks, no matter how high he was. The bullet got its name from the factory in India where it was produced, which also gave the name to the small town near the airport, and, eventually, the airport itself was known as "Dum Dum."